FUTURE PROOF YOUR BUSINESS

AI DIGITAL MARKETING SECRETS

HOW TO LEVERAGE THE POWER OF AI TO INCREASE YOUR SALES, PRODUCTIVITY, EFFICIENCY, PERFORMANCE & CUSTOMER SATISFACTION BY 247%.

ARTIFICIAL INTELLIGENCE & DIGITAL MARKETING ARE <u>INEXTRICABLY</u> LINKED

ANDY BROADAWAY

BEST-SELLING AUTHOR - SPEAKER - AI MARKETING STRATEGIC ADVISOR

AI
DIGITAL MARKETING
SECRETS

© 2023 Copyright Andy Broadaway - All Rights Reserved

Copyright © 2023 by Andy Broadaway. All rights reserved. No part of this publication may be reproduced, distributed, or transmitted in any form or by any means, including photocopying, recording, or other electronic or mechanical methods, without the prior written permission of the publisher, except in the case of brief quotations embodied in critical reviews and certain other noncommercial uses permitted by copyright law. For permission requests, write to the publisher, addressed "Attention: Permissions Coordinator," at: info@abundantpress.com.

Abundant Press www.AbundantPress.com
Ordering Information & Quantity Sales: Special discounts are available on quantity purchases by corporations, associations, and others. For details, contact the publisher. Orders by U.S. & International trade bookstores and wholesalers at: info@abundantpress.com. Printed in the United States of America. Library of Congress-in-Publication Data. Please note: If you find errors, like spelling or grammar, please send us an email.

Title: AI Digital Marketing Secrets
Sub-title: How to leverage the power of AI to increase your sales, productivity, efficiency, performance & customer satisfaction by 247 %
Author: Andy Broadaway
1. The main category of the book — Business, Leadership. Marketing, Sales
ISBN: 978-1-948287-37-1

To Get FREE Access Additional Bonuses Visit:

AiDigitalMarketingSecrets.com

Forward by Denis Waitley

As he does in all of his books, Andy Broadaway stays ahead of the curve of advanced technology to distill for us actionable, clear, real-time strategies to future-proof our careers.

This is a must-read to predict profitable ad campaigns, increase customer buy-in and deliver targeted, compelling content to users.

Only those who internalize and act now to meld digital marketing and breakthroughs in artificial intelligence will survive and thrive in the competitive global marketplace.

Ride the wave of change or be swept aside.

Denis Waitley, Author
The NeuroPsychology of Winning

AI DIGITAL MARKETING SECRETS

Disclaimer: Although the author(s) and publisher have made every effort to ensure that the information in this book was correct at press time. While we try to keep the information up-to-date and accurate, there are no representations or warranties, express or implied, about the completeness, accuracy, reliability, suitability or availability with respect to the information. The author and publisher are NOT providing tax, legal, financial or investment advice, do not assume and hereby disclaim any liability to any party for any loss, damage, or disruption caused by errors or omissions, whether such errors or omissions result from negligence, accident, or any other cause.

Nothing else contained in this book should be used or construed as an offer to sell, a solicitation of an offer to buy, or a recommendation for any security. Nor is it intended as investment, tax, financial or legal advice. Investors should seek such professional advice for their particular situation.

This book is for informational purposes only. This book should not be considered a solicitation, offer or recommendation for the purchase or sale of any securities or other financial products and services discussed herein. Readers of this book will not be considered clients of Andy Broadaway just by virtue of access to this book. Information contained herein is not intended for persons in any jurisdiction where such distribution or use would be contrary to the laws or regulations of that jurisdiction. Readers should not construe any discussion or information contained herein as personalized advice from Andy Broadaway. Neither our information providers nor we shall be liable for any errors or inaccuracies, regardless of cause, or the lack of timeliness of, or for any delay or loss of income.

Certain information contained in this book is derived from sources that Andy Broadaway and/or believes to be reliable; however, Andy Broadaway and/or does not guarantee the accuracy or timeliness of such information and assumes no liability for any resulting damages. Readers should seek advice regarding the appropriateness of investing in any securities or other financial instruments referred to in this book, website or any other message received from Andy Broadaway and should understand that statements regarding future prospects of these or other financial products may not be realized.

Legal Disclosure: You are hereby advised that Andy Broadaway is not a financial advisor and is NOT providing legal or tax advice. Nothing in this book or its attachments should be interpreted by you as legal advice. For legal advice and all legal related matters, Andy Broadaway recommends that you seek the advice of a qualified attorney licensed in your state or jurisdiction

YOUR RIGHTS: This book is restricted to your personal use only. It does not come with any other rights.

AI
DIGITAL MARKETING SECRETS

Table of Contents

INTRODUCTION	1
CHAPTER 1: WHAT IS ARTIFICIAL INTELLIGENCE	7
CHAPTER 2: WHAT IS MACHINE LEARNING	13
CHAPTER 3: WHAT AI CAN DO FOR YOU?	17
CHAPTER 4: HOW TO INCORPORATE AI INTO YOUR BUSINESS	21
CHAPTER 5: YOUR BUSINESS TO THE NEXT LEVEL WITH AI	25
CHAPTER 6: SIGNIFICANCE OF AI IN DIGITAL MARKETING	33
CHAPTER 7: HOW MACHINE LEARNING IS AFFECTING INTERNET MARKETING	47
CHAPTER 8: USE AI TO MAKE SMARTER CAMPAIGNS & LEVERAGE CHATBOTS	51
CHAPTER 9: GOOGLE & AI: HOW ARE THEY ARE USING IT	89
CHAPTER 10: PREPARING FOR SEMANTIC SEARCH	95
CHAPTER 11: SEO & ARTIFICIAL INTELLIGENCE	103
CHAPTER 12: ADVERTISING/ROAS	105
CHAPTER 13: EMAIL MARKETING	113
CHAPTER 14: CASE STUDIES	119
CHAPTER 15: HOW TO FUTURE PROOF YOUR MARKETING	127
CHAPTER 16: WHAT IS CHATGPT?	131
CHAPTER 17: TOOLS AND RESOURCES	143
CHAPTER 18: GLOSSARY OF TERMS	147

Introduction

In terms of both technology and marketing, the world has gone a long way. Artificial intelligence has seamlessly integrated into every aspect of our life, from chatbots to cars that drive themselves.

The number of practical applications for artificial intelligence (AI), as well as the use of products powered by AI has been steadily and rapidly expanding. As the algorithms improve and become more efficient, the capabilities of the various AI products continue to risc.

It is imperative that artificial intelligence become an integral feature of all future digital products.

The field of information technology has developed a passionate obsession with artificial intelligence, sometimes referred to as AI. The use of artificial intelligence is becoming increasingly widespread and has a wide variety of potential applications.

Some examples of these applications include automated customer service and high-end data services.

PC Magazine contributors Rob Marvin and Brian Horowitz note that artificial intelligence (AI) is undeniably becoming a more significant factor in the practical uses of artificial intelligence for your company can take nearly any form, depending on the requirements of your organization and "the business intelligence (BI) insights gained from the data you collect."

AI may be used for a wide variety of tasks, including "mining" social media, automating customer growth and data collection, promoting consumer engagement, optimizing logistics, and improving overall efficiency. In this specialized research, we will take a detailed look at how you may successfully use AI in your company's operations.

However, artificial intelligence has not only revolutionized the realm of technology but has also had a huge effect on marketing.

The question now is, what exactly is the connection between marketing and artificial intelligence? AI is altering what aspects of digital marketing I, and how? Only within the scope of this guide will the answers be provided to all of these queries.

This book will help you learn the significance of artificial intelligence in digital marketing so that you may design a marketing strategy that is more effective.

When it comes to business, having a sharp mind means being aware of what's just around the next bend. It involves having a forward-looking mindset and becoming ready for the inevitable shifts that will have an effect on the way the company is done.

This is what enables a company to be resilient and to flourish in an environment that is always shifting. Digital marketing is no different.

In point of fact, Josh Kaufman, author of The Personal MBA, highlights the advantages of counterfactual simulation in his book of the same name.

This entails visualizing potential outcomes of the future and then making plans to deal with those outcomes. Let's imagine you run a large company that specializes in a field that's doing particularly well for itself there. Perhaps you run a business that offers customers a shake made of whey protein.

The error that some large companies make is to make the assumption that they are too big to fail and to continue operating in the same manner as before.

But imagine if a competing company came up with a superior protein shake that sold for a tenth of the price. What do you think would happen then? What would happen if a previously unknown source of protein was found? What if a study found that consuming whey protein was detrimental to our health?

Any one of these things could take place, and even the most well-established company could be thrown into full disarray as a result. The business, on the other hand, will already have contemplated these possibilities and made preparations for them.

This is an example of a counterfactual simulation, which entails speculating about what's around the corner and then making plans to deal with those potential outcomes.

For those of us working in digital marketing, this means keeping an eye out for trends that might change the face of the industry. And what about one of the things that have the potential to have the most influence of all? Artificial intelligence.

Artificial intelligence (AI) and machine learning have the potential to totally transform the landscape of online marketing, making many of the more traditional marketing methods irrelevant.

You can only guarantee that your websites will maintain their position in the search engine results pages (SERPs), that your advertising campaigns will continue to be successful, and that your services will continue to be relevant if you prepare for those changes in advance.

And a significant portion of this information is not based on conjecture; rather, it is currently taking place. Even if you might not be aware of it just now, AI is already making huge ripples in the industry.

It is having an effect on the operation of SEO, the tools and software that we make use of, as well as the presentation of advertisements. AI is capable of thinking faster and smarter than any person, and this is especially true when it comes to internet marketing, which is a data-driven activity.

Artificial intelligence (AI) can analyze large amounts of data far more efficiently than humans. An AI marketer is capable of producing limitless quantities of content in a split second, effectively accomplishing the work of hundreds of people. Every single piece of content will be ideal when it comes to catering to the target demographic.

AI will manage the company. It will be responsible for managing complete business models. It is going to use AdWords.

Also, it will be able to run brand-new tools that we haven't even thought of yet. The digital marketing singularity is just around the corner.

This book will help you to prepare and explain a number of concepts:

- AI vs Machine Learning
- How to conduct SEO now that Google is an "AI first" company
- Chatbots
- Programmatic advertising
- Digital assistants
- Data science
- Latent Semantic Indexing
- The future of internet marketing

This book I will provide you with a crystal ball that will allow you to look into the future of internet marketing and ensure that you are prepared for all of the changes that are going to occur in the industry. At the conclusion of this guide, you will have gained more knowledge and be in a stronger position than 99.9% of the other marketers.

So, Let's get started

Check out:
AiBrandAccelerator.com

Chapter #1

What is Artificial Intelligence?

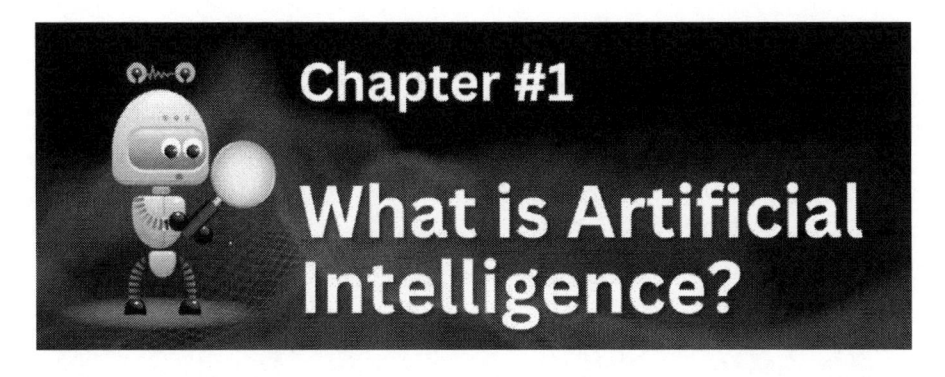

First things first: before we go any further, let's take a look at just what artificial intelligence (AI) and machine learning are. These are two independent concepts that are sometimes mixed up with one another despite their close relationship. Both of these will have an effect on marketing but in distinct and distinct ways.

The simulation of human intelligence processes by machines, most computer systems, is what is referred to as artificial intelligence (AI for short). Expert systems, natural language processing, speech recognition, and machine vision are all examples of specific uses of artificial intelligence.

At this point in time, the amount of data generated by humans and robots combined greatly outpaces the capacity of humans to take in, comprehend, and make difficult choices in relation to the data. Artificial intelligence serves as the foundation for all sorts of computer learning and is the decision-making process of the future.

A comprehension of AI in relation to digital marketing

When used to digital marketing, the use of AI results in increased proficiency due to the automation of operations. AI is also capable of understanding which content is superior and can assist with the curation of content.

As a result, the appropriate material is distributed to the appropriate audience, which results in an increase in ROI.

Artificial intelligence is gaining popularity as a result of the following factors:

- It is much more precision-oriented and permits more reliability and fewer mistakes, leading to increased labor productivity.
- For more pertinent insights, AI examines more and deeper data.
- With its clever algorithms, it can boost the performance of a variety of gadgets. For instance, it includes tracking devices, virtual assistants, and home security systems. With progressive learning algorithms, AI can adapt to new information.

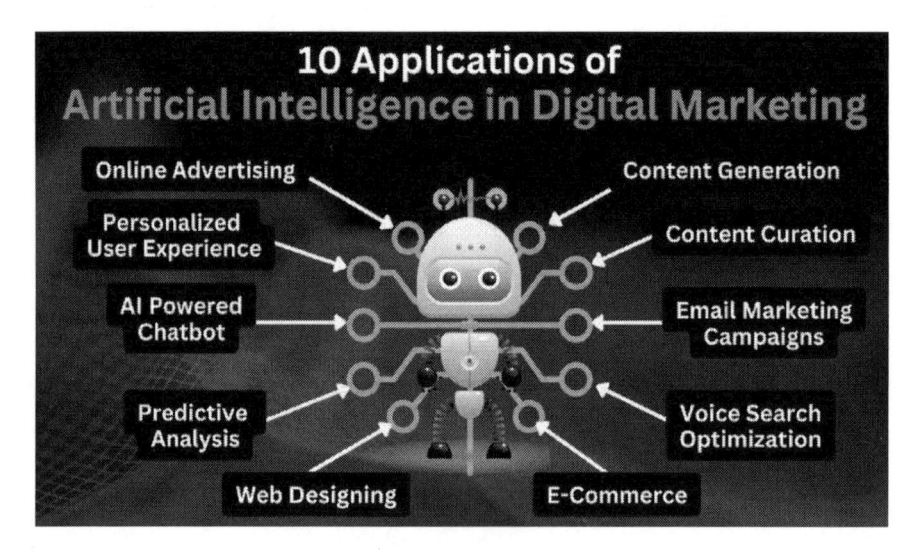

10 Applications of Artificial Intelligence in Digital Marketing

- Online Advertising
- Personalized User Experience
- AI Powered Chatbot
- Predictive Analysis
- Web Designing
- Content Generation
- Content Curation
- Email Marketing Campaigns
- Voice Search Optimization
- E-Commerce

Application of Artificial Intelligence in Digital Marketing

- Before, Digital Marketers were hesitant about using AI in Digital Marketing. Still, with the progress of AI and its results, AI has shown that it is and will bring dynamic changes into the marketing world, and much of the ambiguity has been dissolved.

- **Generating Content** AI can create news and reports based on collected data. Many leading news giants now use automated Journalism.

- **Product Recommendation and Content Curation-** Artificial intelligence can recognize the interest and behavior of the targeted audience and what is better than finding the right products or services that establishments are already seeking.

- **Use of AI Chatbots** – Businesses use automated responses to sort customer queries and data collection, keeping the audience efficient regarding products and services. They can aid clients 24/7 and hold their data for future use.

- **Predictive Analysis-** Artificial Intelligence uses data to make feasible future projections. Predictive analysis is just the use of data, statistical algorithms, and machine learning.

Therefore, AI stands for "artificial intelligence." This refers to both software and technology that have been developed to provide the impression of intelligence. This type of software is able to make meaningful decisions and participate in activities that we would typically regard to be within the purview of humans.

There are two main types of AI to choose from. The first type of AI is known as narrow AI, but it's also known as weak AI. A sort of artificial intelligence that is developed to carry out a certain task is known as weak AI.

The driverless car is a good illustration of this concept. This type of artificial intelligence is capable of recognizing the positions of innumerable cars on the road and acting accordingly by steering, accelerating, and breaking, among other things.

Observing a vehicle that is capable of driving itself from the outside can lead one to believe that a person is behind the wheel. In this respect, it fulfills a function that is traditionally associated with the activities of humans.

But on the other hand, you won't be able to communicate with a self-driving car, so you can't inquire about its emotions either. The Turing Test is not something that could be passed by a car that drives itself!

Note that the Turing test is a test designed to determine how effective artificial intelligence is. It is said that artificial intelligence has "passed the Turing test" if you can have a conversation with it on a chat platform and have no idea that it is not a human being. Another illustration of poor artificial intelligence is shown in the creation of antagonists in video games.

These make use of programming in order to behave in a manner that is similar to that of humans and to present the player with a challenge.

On the other hand, the code is only functional within the framework of the video game, so don't worry about it becoming Skynet any time soon!

Weak artificial intelligence (AI) may not sound as interesting as strong AI, yet it is currently being utilized for a vast variety of highly fascinating tasks, such as helping to treat sickness and boosting the economy.

On the other hand, the kind of artificial intelligence that is frequently depicted in science fiction is referred to as "generic AI." This is a form of artificial intelligence that does not exist to serve a single function but rather is intended to perform all of the tasks that a human being is capable of.

You may, for example, play a word game with this AI, inquire about how it is now feeling, or ask it to dig up some helpful information.

DeepMind, which Google owns, is a good example of a generic artificial intelligence. DeepMind is a startup that has built something called a "neural network," which uses something called "general learning algorithms" to master an extremely wide variety of different abilities.

A large number of artificial intelligence companies, including Watson from IBM, are, in reality, pre-programmed. That entails that they solve problems by employing a process similar to a flow chart and that they will respond to inquiries with the same answer each time.

On the other hand, it would appear that DeepMind is able to think and respond using something called a "convolutional neural network." Certain behaviors are going to be encouraged and reinforced, and as a result, they will start to become more prevalent.

Although this is not an accurate representation of how a human brain operates (cognitive behavioral psychology tells us the significance of having internal dialogues and models for thinking), it is the closest thing we have to a "real" general intelligence at the moment.

Check out:
AiBrandAccelerator.com

Chapter #2
What is Machine Learning?

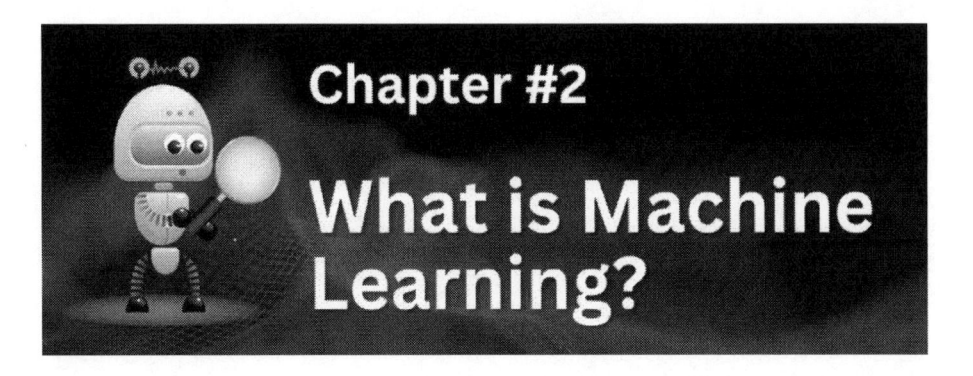

Learning by machine, on the other hand, operates in a different way. The process of machine learning makes use of enormous data sets in order to achieve results that are unexpected and, at times, almost unsettling.

In its most basic form, machine learning makes it possible for a piece of software to be "taught." One clear illustration of this would be the field of computer vision.

The term "computer vision" refers to the capacity that certain types of machines have to comprehend visual information. One such application is Google Lens, which, when used with the camera on a mobile device, can identify whatever it is that the user is looking at, be it a specific species of flower or an item that can be purchased in a shop. Computer vision is essential for autonomous vehicles to be able to traverse their environments successfully. Apps like Snapchat, which utilize filters to modify people's looks, also rely on computer vision to function well.

How does all of this operate? by viewing tens of thousands upon tens of thousands of photographs of each and every kind of thing. Even while the machine learning algorithm will never be able to comprehend the content of the image it is observing; it is able to search for patterns in the data that can be used in the future to recognize the items in question.

For instance, it may observe that faces are often oval-shaped and that they have a black patch of hair on top of their heads. It realizes then that if it observes a shape that is oval with a dark patch at the top, it is most likely looking at a face.

The potential for machine learning to revolutionize virtually every industry is enormous. In the future, it will be possible to use technology to diagnose diseases with greater precision than a human doctor, to provide advice on financial decisions, to detect fraudulent bank transactions, and to do a great deal more besides.

The entirety of this has the potential to have HUGE repercussions for internet marketing, and the latter is the topic that will be covered in the chapters to follow.

The Influence that Machine Learning is Having on Internet Marketing

A significant number of individuals have a limited comprehension of the idea of machine learning. This is not "AI" in the sense that many people conceive of AI; rather, it is a notion in computing that is closely connected to AI. Nevertheless, AI is directly related to this concept.

The term "machine learning" refers to the process by which computers learn, which, in practice, means the process by which computers recognize patterns in enormous data sets.

By looking at thousands of pictures of faces, for instance, a computer can use machine learning to construct face identification algorithms. This can be accomplished by feeding the computer data representing faces. In the end, the system will be able to recognize commonalities in photographs of faces, such as the fact that most faces are oval in shape, that most people have hair, that most faces have contrast points where the eyes belong, etc.

The more information that is input into the system, the more accurate it will be when identifying faces in photographs.

In what ways, then, does this influence online marketing?

Learning From Shopping Behavers

The answer, of course, is that virtually all websites gather large amounts of data as a direct consequence of tracking users. When someone visits a website, Google Analytics and other technologies will keep track of the details of their visit, including the time they arrived, the links they clicked on to get there, the pages they viewed, the time they exited the site, and so on.

All of this information is frequently thrown away. Now, however, with the help of machine learning, it is feasible to transform that data into something that can be used.

When we take a look at the recommendations that Amazon provides, for instance, we notice this. These suggestions are produced as a result of analyzing patterns of behavior exhibited by millions of different clients. When this is done, Amazon's algorithms are able to understand which purchases typically come after others in a customer's shopping history.

Because of this, Amazon is able to reach out to you at just the right moment with just the perfect offer that it thinks you would be interested in, in order to assist you in making a sale!

This is something that we see when we visit the rest of the web as well. Websites are able to communicate with one another and share information because of the cookies that are stored on our computers. Therefore, an advertisement for that same Amazon goods can show up on a website that has nothing to do with it.

In a similar vein, you may be able to determine that a visitor who has arrived at your site from website X is likely to be more interested in purchasing product Y.

For websites that allow users to create accounts, all of this becomes considerably more powerful and effective. These are able to watch the behavior of individuals over extended periods of time, and as a result, far more information regarding their purchasing habits and the likelihood that they would make particular purchases may be gathered.

Machine learning will continue to advance in new and exciting directions from this point forward. At some point in the future, it will be able to modify the structure of a website and display advertisements that are statistically most likely to result in a transaction being made.

In the future, our web surfing experience will constantly be perfectly suited to our particular interests and requirements, based on the information from countless other users' web browsing habits. The end result will be a web that is significantly more effective, as well as, obviously, significantly increased conversions and click-through rates for marketers.

Is that all? Just keep on gathering that information. It's about to come in incredibly handy, don't you worry!

Chapter #3

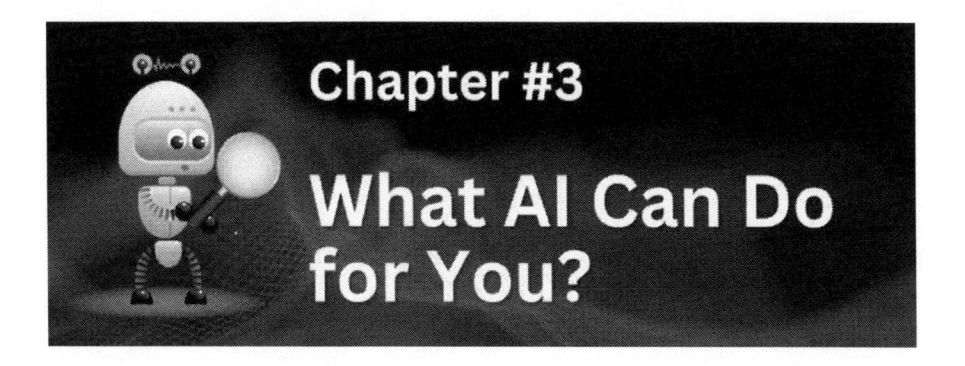

What AI Can Do for You?

According to the findings of a poll of chief executive officers working for companies ranging in size from small to medium-sized (which was carried out by Vistage, a company that provides executive coaching), artificial intelligence is rapidly becoming an important aspect of corporate processes.

According to the results of that study, 29.5% of business leaders said that artificial intelligence, out of all the new technologies, would have the greatest impact on their company in the coming year.

The application of artificial intelligence (AI) and machine learning has already begun in several financial institutions in order to enhance the risk assessment process.

You don't need to go very far into the future to see the benefits that artificial intelligence can provide for you right now.

Tools that are based on AI can provide you with a number of benefits, including the following:

- Lowering costs
- Reducing risk
- Reducing time spent on tasks
- Increasing results
- Improving flexibility and responsiveness

The following are specific areas in which artificial intelligence can assist you with the growth and management of your company: Customer relationship management (CRM) systems are meant to capture customer information from various contact channels like phone, email, and social media.

This information may then be used to improve sales and marketing efforts.

The objective is to contribute to the enhancement and even automation of the sales process.

Platforms such as Salesforce have begun leveraging artificial intelligence to assist small businesses in analyzing the data gleaned from various communication channels, after which they can change their lead generation operations and marketing strategies accordingly.

CRMs that use AI can help businesses produce more leads with the same amount of money spent on marketing. They also demonstrate how artificial intelligence may be utilized to obtain insights that are relevant to marketing and sales, thereby optimizing almost the whole process of customer acquisition.

Communication with customers is being made more automated. On their websites, a variety of small enterprises have recently begun to implement chatbots.

Chatbots have the ability to start discussions and assist with providing answers to client questions. It functions in much the same way as a sales or customer service representative who is available around the clock.

It's highly likely that you've previously interacted with an AI-powered chatbot, even if you didn't recognize it as such at the time. It's the question-and-answer box that appears at the bottom right-hand corner of a website and asks whether you have any issues or questions.

A chatbot could be the solution for your company if you do not yet have a customer care or sales team that is dedicated to your company. This would relieve some of the pressure that you are feeling and allow you to concentrate on the things that are most essential.

Streamlining activities related to human resources —

The sector of human resources is one of the more unexpected places where AI has begun to make an appearance.

It is possible, thanks to the availability of AI tools, to not only make the hiring and "onboarding" process more efficient but also to collect information from new employees that is helpful to HR in improving those processes. Both of these things can have a significant influence on the amount of money you make.

AI can automatically go through all of those applications to locate the people who are the best candidates based on the characteristics you're searching for in an employee.

This can not only increase the likelihood of you discovering the ideal individual, but it can also save you a significant amount of time and resources.
And after the candidate has been hired, the program can assist employees in becoming more knowledgeable about the company's policies and benefits by answering questions they have.

Because you simply do not have the time to sift through all of those applications on your own, this can help you cut down on the amount of time you spend on the hiring process while simultaneously increasing the number of qualified applicants you meet with.

After that, the amount of time spent by HR responding to questions from your new staff is cut down significantly.

Acquiring competitive intelligence—

You've probably entertained fantasies about being able to effortlessly obtain and evaluate information about your competitors, including written and video content, social media posts, and marketing initiatives that assist them in best positioning their business.

The fantastic news is that you won't need to do that because artificial intelligence can handle it for you. There are a number of tools available that will help you keep track of your rivals and the actions they do, including gathering information about them on your behalf and transforming it into reports that are simple to understand.

One example of a tool for analyzing competitors is Crayon, which employs artificial intelligence to monitor competitors across a range of digital platforms, such as their websites and the postings they make on social media.

After that, it will gather a range of information for you, such as minor alterations in the marketing language that they use or changes in the prices that they offer.

These kinds of AI tools make it possible for you to collect more specific information in a shorter amount of time, which enables you to react more quickly and effectively to shifts in the industry that could have an impact on your company.

Check out:
AiBrandAccelerator.com

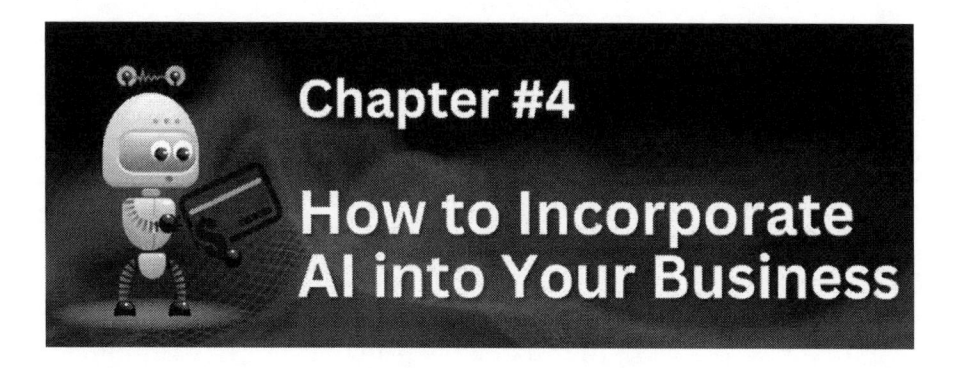

Chapter #4
How to Incorporate AI into Your Business

There are a number of different methods that you may start using AI in your company in order to enhance its exposure and growth.

Here are a few concepts to consider:

Learn about artificial intelligence (AI) and what it's capable of doing.

Because it collaborates with other institutions, such as Stanford University, as well as "corporations in the AI field," Luke Tang's TechCode Accelerator is able to provide you with access to a diverse range of resources.

Make the most of the wealth of material that is currently available to you and become acquainted with the fundamental ideas behind artificial intelligence.

Some of the workshops and online classes that are provided by organizations such as Udacity come highly recommended by Tang himself.

You won't have any trouble getting started with these simple approaches to artificial intelligence, and they will assist you in expanding your knowledge of topics such as machine learning and predictive analytics.

Here are some resources you can use to get started (not all are free):

- Udacity's "Intro to AI" course and their Artificial Intelligence Nanodegree Program.
- Stanford University's online lectures: Artificial Intelligence, Principles & Techniques.
- Microsoft's open-source "Cognitive Toolkit" (previously called CNTK) to help master deep-learning algorithms.
- Google's open-source "TensorFlow" software library for machine intelligence.
- AI Resources, an open-source code directory from the AI Access Foundation.

To get started, you will need to determine the issues that you want artificial intelligence to fix for you.

After you have a firm grasp on the fundamentals, the next step is to begin investigating and coming up with new ideas.

You should immediately begin considering how you can integrate AI into the products and services you already offer. It's likely that you've already thought of particular scenarios in which artificial intelligence could help you address some of the challenges you face or deliver clear benefits to your organization.

Streamlining the employment process or providing better support to clients by way of question-and-answer sessions.

According to Tang, "when we're dealing with a company, we start by getting an overview of its most important technology programs and difficulties." We want to be able to show it how natural language processing, picture recognition, machine learning, and other similar technologies fit into those goods, and the best way to do so is typically through some kind of workshop with the company's management. The particulars shift constantly from sector to sector.

For instance, if the company is involved in video monitoring, adding machine learning to the process can help the organization capture a significant amount of additional value.

Prioritize value.

Your next step is to take some time to sit down and conduct an analysis of the potential value, both in terms of your company's operations and its finances, of the artificial intelligence implementations that you are considering introducing into your company.

Tang places a strong emphasis on the significance of ensuring that one does not get lost in discussion of "pie in the sky," but rather that one links one's endeavors directly to sound business ideals.

This way, you won't allow yourself to become sidetracked by all the possibilities, but rather, you'll focus on achieving something that is within your reach.

According to Tang, the process of prioritizing involves looking at the dimensions of potential and practicality and placing them into a two-by-two matrix. You should be able to prioritize based on near-term visibility using this information, and you should also be able to determine the financial value of the organization.

In most cases, you will require the ownership and recognition of managers and top-level executives in order to proceed with this phase.

Recognize the areas in which you lack capability.

What you want to achieve for your company and what you are actually capable of achieving within a given amount of time are two very different things, and there is a significant gap between the two.

Before diving headfirst into a comprehensive artificial intelligence endeavor, a company should, in Tang's opinion, first determine "from a tech and business process standpoint" what it is and is not capable of achieving.

He notes that "this can sometimes take a long time to do." [Citation needed] "Identifying what you need to acquire and any processes that need to be internally involved before you begin underway is the first step in addressing the capability gap that exists within your organization,"

Depending on the company, there may be ongoing initiatives or teams that can lend a hand in achieving this goal in a natural way for specific business units.

Check out:
AiBrandAccelerator.com

Chapter #5
Your Business to the Next Level with AI

Participation from all members of staff is necessary if you want to transition your company into an AI-driven environment. You can also begin the process today, despite the fact that it will take some time to convert the organization.

The transformation of your organization's culture into one that welcomes experimentation, information, and agile principles is one step that can be taken.

To successfully transition to a digital world, you will need to automate more than simply a few tasks. You have to integrate that digital ecosystem so that it can penetrate and develop every action that is carried out within your firm.

Artificial intelligence is no longer something that only the Fortune 500 can afford. The market for artificial intelligence is being entered by an increasing number of sole proprietors, sole proprietorships, and small corporations.

You will be able to improve your company decisions and grow in relevance with the assistance of analytics, which helps you transform information into intelligence.

AI may assist in the development of superior marketing tactics and assist in gaining a deeper understanding of your clientele. One of the most lucrative applications of artificial intelligence is the ability to evaluate information in order to enhance sales.

The algorithms that make up artificial intelligence are able to sift through vast amounts of user data in search of trends and patterns. Additionally, this can result in more successful marketing and contribute to the development of your content strategy.

According to a study conducted at Harvard University, searching through chat logs in search of relevant terms and phrases that correlate with successful sales can increase your success rates by as much as 54 percent.

Activity on social media can provide artificial intelligence systems, such as the recommendation system used by Amazon, with sufficient information to identify purchasing habits for particular customers.

Artificial intelligence that monitors behavior is being used by Amazon's CEO of Worldwide Consumers, Jeff Wilke, instead of the more traditional marketing algorithms that are based on people's memories.

The pricing of goods and services can also be influenced by AI. An algorithm can monitor trends to assist in determining your ideal prices, which can then be used to maximize your profit margins.

Algorithms powered by artificial intelligence can also be used to replace humans in a range of menial jobs, which frees up more time, resources, and money that can be put to other purposes.

Even though this might not sound like good news to some people (robot apocalypse, anyone?), the majority of business owners have a more pragmatic outlook on the situation.

An artificial intelligence can be a very helpful adjunct to a human worker.

When it comes to administrative labor, artificial intelligence can whiz through it, freeing up your employees to focus on more creative endeavors and on parts of your company that are more crucial to its success.

Your staff will be able to put their skills and efforts to greater use if they are freed from performing simple activities that can be done more readily by AI.

You probably wouldn't believe that artificial intelligence could understand human feelings, but the technology actually has some surprising uses, including something called "sentiment analysis."

Sentiment analysis algorithms may create some pretty accurate predictions about human attitudes to specific issues by utilizing picture recognition software, polls, social media, and even more ways.

This technology has been around for some time, and it was even utilized during the election campaign that President Obama ran in 2012 in order to gauge how the general public felt about certain policy announcements made by him.

Your company's ability to accurately predict the behavior of your customers and to respond in real time to shifting marketing trends are both made possible by sentiment analysis.

Enhancing your company's day-to-day operations can also help your company develop more quickly. The "heavy lifting" that you need done can be done by AI algorithms, and they are ready and prepared to do it.

The use of artificial intelligence allows for analysis of processes such as workflows and supply chains to identify areas that could be improved.

By streamlining your workflow, you may ensure that resources are used more effectively, hence reducing the expenses associated with maintenance, lost time, and redundancy.

The implementation of artificial intelligence is likely to be beneficial to organizations in the manufacturing sector. According to Forbes magazine, material operations that make use of artificial intelligence have the potential to see a 20% boost in production capacity while also experiencing a 4% decline in the number of materials required.

What are the Different Ways That AI Can Be Integrated into Digital Marketing Strategies?

The application of artificial intelligence (AI) has significantly altered the methods in which businesses operate. Not only does it make it easier for businesses to run efficiently, but it also adds value by freeing up time for businesses to concentrate on coming up with innovative and original answers to problems.

The field of digital marketing is likewise being significantly impacted by AI in a significant way. Artificial intelligence can be incorporated into digital marketing strategy in a variety of effective ways.

Chatbots A conversational or text-based software program that uses artificial intelligence to determine its responses is called a chatbot. It's possible that people used a chatbot on a website to find the answers they were looking for when they had a question.

There will not be any marketing done by a chatbot that is sent out into the public. It is nothing at all like the type of marketing channel that has been utilized in the past, such as advertisements or email messages.

However, practical marketing tools such as chatbots, which are primarily used on social media platforms, can facilitate user service, which benefits both the user and their brand. Additionally, these tools can collect data on customers, which enables businesses to target their messaging and deliver those targeted messages.

Content that is Predictive and Tailored to the Audience
In addition, AI can collect additional data on users and prospects in order to provide answers to questions posed by chatbots.

This data can be used by AI to make predictions about future behavior as well as to produce targeted messaging. It's possible that a chatbot will offer that content by email, or by dynamic range on a website.

This is due to the fact that AI can provide assistance in sending the appropriate email message at the appropriate time by utilizing dynamic content and selecting that material based on previous actions taken by customers.

Here Are Three Suggestions That Will Help You Make Successful Use of AI

First and foremost, don't forget to factor storage space into your plan.

When expanding from a small data sample, it is important to keep in mind the storage requirements that will be necessary, according to Philip Pokorny, Chief Technical Officer at Penguin Computing, which provides solutions in the areas of high-performance computing, artificial intelligence, and machine learning.

In his article titled "Critical Decisions: A Guide to Building the Complete Artificial Intelligence Solution Without Regrets," he made the statement that "Improving algorithms is vital to obtaining research findings."

"However, artificial intelligence systems are unable to advance to the point where they can accomplish your computing goals without access to enormous volumes of data that can assist in the construction of more accurate models.

Because of this, the incorporation of storage that is both quick and well-optimized should be considered right from the beginning of the design process for AI systems.

Additionally, he recommends that you optimize the storage used for artificial intelligence for "data input, workflow, and modeling." When the system is live, taking the time to carefully consider your options can have a significant and beneficial effect on the way it operates.

The second piece of advice is to include AI into your business.

According to Dominic Wellington, Global IT Evangelist at Moogsoft, if you want to make artificial intelligence a part of your daily routine rather than trying to completely replace that routine with AI, you have a tool at your disposal that can take advantage of the additional automation and insight offered by AI (a provider of AI for IT operations).

According to him, "some employees may be apprehensive of technology that can disrupt their job." Because of this, it is essential to present the solution as a means to augment the employees' daily responsibilities.

He also adds that you should be upfront with your employees about how technology works to fix challenges in your workflow. This is something that he recommends you do.

"This offers employees an 'under the hood' experience so that they can clearly understand how AI augments their function rather than removing it," he adds. "This gives employees an 'under the hood' experience so that they can clearly visualize how AI augments their position."

Tip #3: Balance, balance, balance.

Pokorny emphasizes that in order to successfully design an artificial intelligence system, one must not only fulfill the requirements of the technology but also those of the research project; hence, one must carefully balance their construction efforts.

Even before beginning the process of designing an AI system, according to Pokorny, the most important thing to keep in mind is to ensure that the system is built with balance.

This may sound like a no-brainer, but far too often, artificial intelligence (AI) systems are designed around specific aspects of how the team envisions achieving its research goals, without understanding the requirements and limitations of the hardware and software that would support the research. This is a problem because it prevents the team from designing AI systems that are optimal for the research.

The end result is a system that is less than optimal and even dysfunctional, and it is unable to do what it set out to do.

In order to achieve a state of equilibrium inside your system, you will need to ensure that there is sufficient bandwidth for storage, networking, the graphics processing unit (GPU), and security.

In order for artificial intelligence to perform its functions effectively, it must have access to enormous amounts of data. You need to make sure that you have a good understanding of the different types of data that will be involved with your project, and you also need to be aware that the standard security measures that you use (such as anti-malware software, encryption, and virtual private networks, or VPN) may not be sufficient.

Your computer's vulnerability to potential security breaches increases in proportion to the amount of interaction it has with the wider world.

In a similar vein, according to Pokorny, "you have to strike a balance between the necessity to defend against power failure and other scenarios through redundancy and the way in which the entire money is spent to accomplish research."

It's possible that you'll also need to design your system so that it's flexible enough to accommodate repurposing of hardware in response to shifting user needs.

Chapter #6: Significance of AI in Digital Marketing

What is the connection between digital marketing and artificial intelligence?

AI is able to develop simulation models and customize purchasing processes by making recommendations based on technologies for machine learning and interacting with virtual assistants.

Why is artificial intelligence so crucial in digital marketing?

AI is taking over the function formerly played by humans in identifying trends in marketing because of its more in-depth research, data analysis, and input. In an effort to reduce the amount of time and resources expended, marketers and brands are beginning to implement artificial intelligence and machine learning.

Help the Speaker Better Understand the Audience by Providing the Following:

AI may assist in the analysis of data with the goal of simplifying it; it can also foresee the purchasing patterns and decisions of targeted audiences; and it can enhance the user experience in order to provide those audiences what they want.

More Efficient Marketing: The corporation is now able to develop a marketing strategy for the company that is more efficient thanks to the data-driven analysis provided by AI.

Boost Productivity: The company can automate a large number of time-consuming, repetitive jobs thanks to AI. This contributes to the improvement of the overall level of production.

AI makes it possible to make decisions and also contributes to the production of material that performs better, which helps to increase ROI (return on investment).

What Differences Will the Future of AI Make to Digital Marketing?

There are hundreds of different fields in which artificial intelligence is causing significant shifts. The field of artificial intelligence is rapidly expanding, and many companies now conduct their operations in the financial and technological sectors. These are some examples of how AI is shaping Digital Marketing:

1. Marketing that is directed for a very specific audience

Convincing potential customers is an essential component of targeted marketing. But how can organizations get people to believe that they are ignorant of something? With the help of artificial intelligence (AI), virtual assistants, predictive consumer segmentation, or intelligent design for tailored customer experiences can be created.

2. Marketing that is both personalized and automated

It is possible for companies to gain a major edge in the competition for customers, which will result in an increase in sales revenue during the period following the epidemic. Automation of pay-per-click (PPC) ads, display ads, conversion rates, search engine marketing (SEM), keyword research, search engine optimization (SEO), and social media marketing are some of the marketing tasks that can be assisted by AI technology.

Utilizing AI to Make Predictions Regarding Customers' Behavior

Businesses stand to gain a great deal from implementing AI due to its many useful applications. It is able to forecast the behavior of customers, which is one of its primary features.

It is to your advantage to have as much information as possible regarding the behavior of your clients. You may provide a higher level of customer service by utilizing behavior data, and you can also utilize these insights to better sell your services.

The question now is, how exactly can AI forecast the behavior of customers? Continue reading to discover.

How exactly does AI predict the behavior of customers?

The purpose of artificial intelligence (AI) technology is to do data analysis and intelligent decision making based on what it has learned. It is an extremely complicated piece of technology that, as the years go by, continues to acquire more and more intelligence.

It takes into consideration a wide variety of information, such as previous purchases, consumer requests, and expectations. From that point on, it is able to produce a prediction of future client behavior that is eerily accurate.

What are the Advantages of Doing This?

Utilizing AI to make predictions about the actions of one's customers can result in a number of positive outcomes. The most important ones are as follows:

- Increases client happiness
- Contributes to the enhancement of marketing efforts;
- Contributes to cost reductions and enhanced earnings

According to a number of studies, the application of the appropriate AI technology has the potential to increase levels of customer satisfaction by as much as 10%.

Because it generates accurate forecasts, you will be able to sell your goods and services more effectively as a result. Customers will receive recommendations for personalized products, and it will let you know which marketing strategies will result in the highest revenue for your business.

Investing in the appropriate AI technology will also help you reduce expenses. Because it makes accurate predictions of behavior, you won't squander money selling things that don't work. You won't just know the general location of your clients, but you'll also know exactly where to concentrate your advertising efforts.

This has the potential to save an incredible amount of money. You'll notice that your profits go up as a result of the greater conversion rates you achieve as a result of the fact that it helps you produce warmer leads.

When you utilize AI to forecast the behavior of your customers, you may anticipate these as some of the primary benefits.

Businesses are able to create adverts that are savvier and more specific when they use AI. Artificial intelligence is in a position to positively effect global trends on a bigger scale, as well as sustainability and scalability.

1. Enhancements to Both the Personalization and Recommendation Systems

The use of AI now enables marketers to personalize their communications on a consumer-centric level, as opposed to the general target groups on which they previously relied. This technology forecasts the behavior of customers by drawing on the knowledge gained from their previous experiences with a brand.

The majority of people are going to already be familiar with the individualized suggestions that are available whenever a user goes into a website such as Amazon or Netflix. Over the course of their existence, these recommendation engines have steadily gained in level of sophistication.

They have the potential to be astonishingly accurate, particularly for clients who have maintained an account for a number of years, which enables the service to compile a substantial amount of information over time.

As an illustration, Amazon keeps a record of everything a consumer has ever purchased from them.

- The user's surfing history
- The addresses at which the user lived and worked
- Items that the user desired to purchase
- The television shows and music that the user played
- The applications that the user downloaded
- Product ratings and reviews that the user has written and left
- The electronic devices that customers employed in order to watch movies or download eBooks
- Everything that the user requested Alexa

2. SEO (Optimization for Search Engines)

Search engines like Google, which are used by millions of people on a daily basis, have improved their search algorithms, which means that smaller database product searches on e-commerce sites are also benefiting from these advancements.

AI is vital for interpreting complicated speech patterns and extracting meaning from spoken search queries, which are substantially different from the typical typed searches that are performed.

Marketers can also use AI to optimize their content for voice search, which can help improve SEO and site traffic as we move increasingly toward a voice-operated digital environment.

Marketers can use AI to optimize their content for voice search.

3. Establishing Dynamic Pricing

It is possible to utilize AI to dynamically determine the price of products in accordance with parameters such as demand, availability, client profiles, and other considerations in order to maximize sales and profits.

4. Providing Service to Customers Chatbots

Chatbots are able to be programmed to deliver predetermined responses to questions that are posed on a regular basis and to transfer the conversation to a human agent if the subject is too complicated for the chatbot to answer.

Chatbots are not only more cost-effective than recruiting more team members to deal with enquiries, but they also have the potential to handle the task in a more effective and even more "human" manner at times. Because, unlike people, machines never have a bad day, you can depend on them to behave in a way that is courteous, interesting, and endearing at all times.

5. Scalable Methods of Content Production and Curation

The return on investment that can be made through content marketing is rather significant. However, it is also possible for it to be "resource heavy."

There are multiple ways in which artificial intelligence (AI) might help speed up and optimize content marketing.

Automated content software can now create news stories and reports in a matter of seconds, whereas previously, it would have taken human authors minutes, hours, or even days to develop such content.

There are now a number of global companies publishing content that was at least partially generated by AI.

1. Automatically Generate Content

Marketers working in the field of artificial intelligence are able to utilize software that allows them to automatically generate content for straightforward narratives such as stock market updates and sports reports. Even if the text is read to you by an algorithm, it is still possible for it to be traced without your knowledge.

2. Make use of chatbots to engage in conversation with users

Artificial intelligence can be utilized to simulate conversations with customers through the usage of chatbots. A good example of this is Facebook Messenger, which makes use of chatbots to simulate interactions with specific demographics of users by providing real-time responses to their questions and concerns.

3. Algorithms for Personalized News Feeds

The news feeds of users on social media platforms such as Facebook, Twitter, and Instagram can now be personalized thanks to artificial intelligence. Because of this, people will only see the posts that are relevant to them.

Taking on the Obstacles that Have Been Placed

Despite the fact that artificial intelligence technology can provide a great deal of benefits in terms of predicting the actions of customers, it also comes with a great deal of difficulties.

To begin, it is not something that can be grasped quickly. Because of this, many companies choose to delay incorporating it into their operations for the time being. They think it would be too difficult for them to add it themselves. You can, on the other hand, apply the technology on your own if you have the appropriate AI technology strategy. Therefore, if you have been hesitating because you believe it will be too difficult to implement, now is the time to start conducting research and formulating a strategy for doing so.

The price tag represents yet another possible obstacle. There is no way to get around the fact that artificial intelligence technologies can be quite pricey. Having said that, you must take into consideration the cost benefits over a longer period of time.

There are also many subcategories within the field of artificial intelligence technology. You should therefore be able to locate an alternative that is less expensive to begin with.

The use of AI technology to the task of predicting the actions of customers can result in a number of beneficial outcomes. These are just some of the many ways that it can be beneficial to your company. Having stated that, it is important to conduct adequate study before introducing artificial intelligence (AI) technology into the business.

When you have a deeper understanding of the technology, it will be much simpler for you to incorporate it into the company.

How can AI be used, and what roles does it play, in digital marketing?

Artificial intelligence is playing an increasingly important role in digital marketing, and this trend is expected to continue at an exponential rate. These are the roles that artificial intelligence plays and the uses that it has in digital marketing.

1. The process of data collection, recognition, and analysis

Management of a company's interactions with its customers, often known as CRM, is essential to maintaining healthy relationships with those customers. It has a tendency to recognize the requirements for taking a business approach that is centered on the user. The use of AI technology makes it possible to efficiently collect customer data from a variety of platforms, acquire insights from that data, and target audiences based on the requirements of those audiences.

2. AI in conjunction with AR and VR

An extraordinary adventure is attainable through the utilization of artificial intelligence, augmented reality (AR), and virtual reality (VR).

Users are able to communicate with one another and discover more information about a brand in interesting new ways. In addition to this, it helps contribute to the identity of the brand, which in turn increases both awareness of the brand and loyalty to it.

The use of artificial intelligence in digital marketing has been revolutionized by the automation of email marketing. Emails sent to customers by marketers can be customized to reflect the actions those customers have taken in the past.

The Role of AI in the Development of the Digital Marketing Industry

The digital landscape of today is being reshaped in significant ways by artificial intelligence. AI is replacing humans in the job of identifying marketing trends by performing data analysis in the real world and having the ability to react to new information.

As a direct consequence of this, brands and marketers are increasingly turning to AI for usage in digital marketing in order to cut down on wasted time and costs by utilizing automated digital marketing services.

1. A more individualized approach to marketing:

As AI continues to advance, algorithms will be able to understand the psychology of individuals and their needs based on the activities they engage in on social media. This will make it possible to approach marketing in a manner that is more individualized. Only people who have a real need for a company's goods and services will attract investment from that company.

2. A more engaging and individualized approach to customer service

The customer service would take on a more engaging and individual approach. Client service software such as chatbots is capable of doing a wide variety of tasks, including responding to customer inquiries, delivering information regarding products and services, and generating sales.

3. Convenient tools for looking for products and receiving recommendations

Searching for products and receiving recommendations would be more particular. Voice search has reached its pinnacle thanks to the development of artificial intelligence.

4. Highly developed methods of processing

For analyzing data Machine learning algorithms have emerged independently because to the fact that humans are unable to analyze enormous amounts of data effectively.

The reasons why AI will alter the course of digital marketing in the future

The following is a list of the top five reasons why artificial intelligence is affecting the future of digital marketing:

What role artificial intelligence is playing in the field of digital marketing.

1. Increases One's Awareness

Have you ever pondered the reasons why brands choose not to advertise? A recent survey found that 71 percent of people who work in marketing believe that firms fail to know their customer base. Sixty-six percent of marketers have expressed the desire for brands to place a greater emphasis on cultivating users' awareness and relationships.

It makes it easier to create reminders and alerts, and it provides clear and precise answers when they are needed, all thanks to an AI-based voice assistant, technology, and the Internet of Things.

2. Make use of the Internet of Things.

The power of the internet of things and the devices that are connected to it is being leveraged by AI, which is another significant reason why AI is reshaping the future of digital marketing. When all you need is your phone, and it works from anywhere, that is a major leap from the way things were in the past.

The influence that artificial intelligence (AI) will have on digital marketing

Within a relatively short period of time, artificial intelligence will have a significant impact on the field of digital marketing.

There is little doubt that AI and machine learning will shake up the digital marketing industry in a variety of different ways.

How Artificial Intelligence Affects the Digital Marketing Industry

1. Marketing Using Predictive Models

A method known as predictive marketing is one that determines which marketing efforts will be most effective in a specific circumstance. This is achieved by the AI assistant performing data analytics in order to decide the marketing tactics and actions that have the best likelihood of being successful.

Artificial intelligence will make predictive marketing more accessible and easier to manage, despite the fact that predictive marketing has been around for quite some time.

There is little question that businesses who use predictive marketing to make data-driven decisions will have much improved results.

This approach, which is driven by data, would enable businesses generate data-based predictions about: how customers would make purchases; when customers would make purchases; and how customers would make those purchases.

Based on their previous actions, how many customers have indicated that they would spend money?

2. Personalization

AI will assist businesses in developing marketing strategies and advertisements that are even more specifically tailored to the needs of their leads and customers.

The most up-to-date strategies for digital marketing already incorporate a significant amount of personalization.

The company is equipped with the resources and technology necessary to discriminate between users based on a variety of factors, including gender, age, interests, previous browsing history, and more. For instance, the standard procedure these days is for one target group to view a different assortment of headlines and photographs than another target group. However, the process of personalization in digital marketing is just getting started.

Check out:
AiBrandAccelerator.com

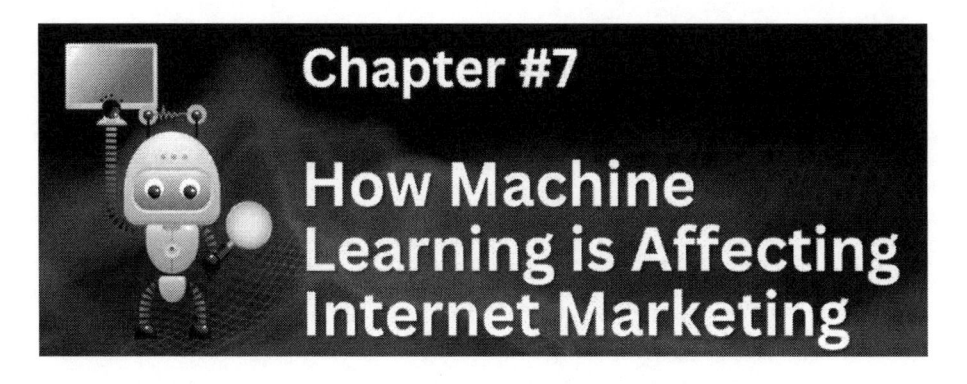

Chapter #7
How Machine Learning is Affecting Internet Marketing

A significant number of individuals have a limited comprehension of the idea of machine learning. This is not "AI" in the sense that many people conceive of AI; rather, it is a notion in computing that is closely connected to AI. Nevertheless, AI is directly related to this concept.

The term "machine learning" refers to the process by which computers learn, which, in practice, means the process by which computers recognize patterns in enormous data sets.

By looking at thousands of pictures of faces, for instance, a computer can use machine learning to construct face identification algorithms. This can be accomplished by feeding the computer data representing faces. In the end, the system will be able to recognize commonalities in photographs of faces, such as the fact that most faces are oval in shape, that most people have hair, that most faces have contrast points where the eyes belong, etc.

The more information that is input into the system, the more accurate it will be when identifying faces in photographs. **In what ways, then, does this influence online marketing?**

The Lessons Learned from Shopping Behaviour
The answer, of course, is that large amounts of data are gathered by virtually all websites as a direct consequence of tracking users.

When someone visits a website, Google Analytics and other technologies will keep track of the details of their visit, including the time they arrived, the links they clicked on to get there, the pages they viewed, the time they exited the site, and so on.

All of this information is frequently thrown away. Now, however, with the help of machine learning, it is feasible to transform that data into something that can be used.

When we take a look at the recommendations that Amazon provides, for instance, we notice this. These suggestions are produced as a result of analysing the behavior patterns exhibited by millions of different clients. When this is done, Amazon's algorithms are able to understand which purchases typically come after others in a customer's shopping history.

Because of this, Amazon is able to reach out to you at just the right moment, with just the perfect offer that it thinks you would be interested in, in order to assist you in making a sale!

This is something that we see when we visit the rest of the web as well. Websites are able to communicate with one another and share information because of the cookies that are stored on our computers. Therefore, an advertisement for that same Amazon goods can show up on a website that has nothing to do with it.

In a similar vein, you may be able to determine that a visitor who has arrived at your site from website X is likely to be more interested in purchasing product Y.

For websites that allow users to create accounts, all of this becomes considerably more powerful and effective. These are able to watch the behavior of individuals over extended periods of time, and as a result, far more information regarding their purchasing habits and the likelihood that they would make particular purchases may be gathered.

Machine learning will continue to advance in new and exciting directions from this point forward. At some point in the future, it will be able to modify the structure of a website and display advertisements that are statistically most likely to result in a transaction being made.

In the future, our web surfing experience will constantly be perfectly suited to our particular interests and requirements, based on the information from countless other users' web browsing habits. The end result will be a web that is significantly more effective, as well as, obviously, significantly increased conversions and click-through rates for marketers.

Is that all? Just keep on gathering that information. It's about to come in incredibly handy, don't you worry!

Check out:
AiBrandAccelerator.com

Chapter #8
Use AI to Make Smarter Campaigns & leverage Chatbots

The term "programmatic advertising" has been in use for some time, but huge corporations employ it more frequently than online marketers do at this point.

This is a mistake, however, because programmatic advertising has the potential to be enormously beneficial for any marketing campaign. Programmatic advertising can achieve this by leveraging the considerable power of artificial intelligence in order to run advertising campaigns that are more intelligent.

What exactly is meant by the term programmatic advertising?

A style of advertising known as programmatic advertising is one that makes use of an algorithm in order to put advertisements on a selection of a variety of different platforms. It is possible for businesses to invest a significant amount of time and effort into collaborating with a variety of publishers and advertising platforms in order to increase the number of people who see their advertisements.

Not only does this take a lot of time, but it also has the potential to result in money being lost. This is due to the fact that you run the risk of having to pay for an advertisement that receives no clicks and, as a result, does not bring in any revenue for your business.

The programmatic approach seeks to alter all of this by managing everything on your behalf. You will only need to create a single advertisement because the tool will see to it that it is published on the very finest websites.

However, maybe of more significance is the fact that programmatic advertising is highly optimized. This is due to the fact that it will utilize algorithms that learn through machine learning to discover important aspects of your campaign and match those aspects with the platforms and publications.

To put it another way, programmatic advertising platforms are able to determine the age, gender, and interests of your typical consumer and then use that knowledge to position your adverts in locations where those specific types of people are likely to view them.

Because of this, your advertisements will be highly targeted, which means that the individuals who see them will have a greater chance of clicking on them and making a purchase from you.

In addition to this, a programmatic advertising tool will have the ability to adapt to new circumstances and develop over time. If an advertisement is not doing well enough, for instance, it may be removed from that placement.

Programmatic buying allows marketers to spend less time engaging with publishers and to optimize their campaigns by integrating automation and machine learning. This gives programmatic buying a competitive advantage.

Programmatic: A Guide to Your Own Success

Even though programmatic advertising will take care of a significant portion of the process for you, there are still a few things that you need to keep in mind if you want to get the most out of this effective technique.

To begin, you need to make sure that the advertisement you create is interesting to people, noticeable, and appropriate for the people who will be viewing it.

However, because your advertisements have the potential to be displayed in a wide variety of settings, it is essential that you create them in such a way that they are adaptable. Your advertisements should have an appealing appearance regardless of whether they are displayed as banner ads on a personal blog or are dispersed over a large website.

In conclusion, you shouldn't be scared to spend some money right off the get. Programmatic advertising, like any data-driven strategy, is centred on gathering as much information as is practically possible.

Your strategy will get more refined and effective the more errors you make while implementing it.

How a Chatbot Could Boost Traffic and Sales

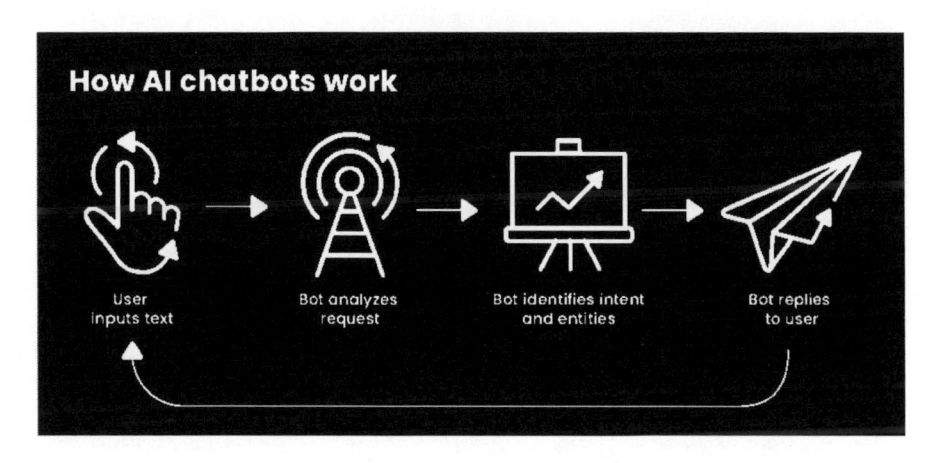

A chatbot is essentially a small piece of artificial intelligence that will often reside on a website and will have the ability to respond to questions and carry-on simple conversations with users.

In the world of customer service, chatbots are becoming increasingly common. A website can reduce the workload of its customer care personnel by a large amount by providing answers to queries that are often inquired about on the site.

The organization is able to provide the service it desires to for its customers, even without having to invest a significant amount of money on additional members of staff or contact centers.

However, a chatbot's capabilities extend far beyond providing simple customer service. When it comes to marketing, chatbots are just as effective, and they have the potential to be incredibly beneficial in terms of increasing sales and profitability. Chatbots are particularly useful for getting a sales process off the ground. They do this by greeting visitors to a website and inquiring as to what they are looking for on the site.

Instead of depending on user experience (UX) to try and steer the visitor to the appropriate section of the page, a chatbot can instead just ask what the visitor is looking to purchase, and then take them to the page that corresponds to that product or service.

In addition to this, it is able to present customers with helpful recommendations (which may be gleaned from their past purchasing history) and it can alleviate any fears that consumers may have.

Customers can even provide information to chatbots by answering questions about their preferences and budgets. Chatbots can even ask customers what they are looking for.

Even if they don't make a purchase, you now have a better understanding of their motives, and you can put this knowledge to use in refining your marketing plan. It has been speculated that chatbots will be responsible for 85 percent of all corporate transactions within the next several years.

The question now is, how will you begin?

Eighty percent of organizations have expressed an interest in implementing chatbots by the year 2022.

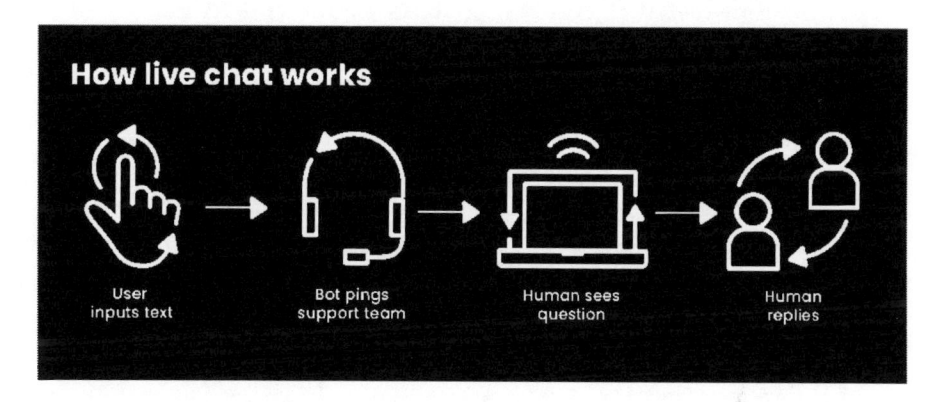

How live chat works

User inputs text → Bot pings support team → Human sees question → Human replies

Chatbots available on Facebook

Purchasing a chatbot that operates on Facebook is one of your options. There is a plethora of websites and services available on the internet that will configure these for you.

Many locally owned and operated companies view Facebook Messenger as an uncharted territory. In spite of the fact that many marketers have failed to notice it, the data clearly demonstrate its significance.

Over one billion and two hundred million people are currently using Facebook Messenger. That amounts to 11% of the total population of humans.

The fact that Messenger may be integrated into a website is another feature that contributes to its already impressive functionality. Over twenty million pages currently make use of messaging, and that number is only expected to expand. This makes it incredibly simple and convenient to engage with your site's visitors, to respond to their inquiries, and to assist in converting site traffic into sales.

However, it is impossible to meet the requirements of all of your guests if you are present around the clock. A chatbot can replace human interaction in this situation. This is a simple artificial intelligence that can assist you in taking care of your consumers and helping to give a more personalized experience while answering basic inquiries.

Because of this incredibly useful tool for businesses, you will no longer lose customers because they were unable to navigate your website or get the information they required. This is a major advantage over your competitors. Imagine if customers were able to place orders for food by just sending a message on Facebook and then responding to a few questions posed by an automated system.

Or, what if a company could get access to your skilled legal counsel without ever having to have a face-to-face conversation with you? The immediate future holds the potential for all of these things.

Facebook chatbots even have the ability to convey messages to prospective customers before they engage with them. Because this has the potential to be interpreted as spam, you need to exercise utmost caution when dealing with it.

However, if you have an automated system that is able to reach out to prospective customers at the exact appropriate time with a message that has been carefully designed, this can be quite beneficial for your company.

Additional Varieties of Chatbots

It should be noted that Facebook chatbots are not the only type of chatbot. It is possible to integrate chatbots into a website in a variety of various ways, such as building them from the ground up using custom software or programming them to respond to incoming emails or text messages.

Get a chatbot if you want to move your website into the 21st century, maybe raise your sales, and improve client satisfaction all at the same time.

You have almost certainly come across the term "chatbot." You could also be familiar with the concept of a chatbot; perhaps you are aware that it is connected in some way to either AI or machine learning.

You may also be aware that it is a means through which companies can interact directly with millions of customers despite the absence of their physical presence.

In my booked titled: **"If eMail Marketing is Dead, what's next"**

I talk extensively about Chatbots and their role.

The question now is, what precisely is a chatbot?

What are they doing there? In what ways might they be beneficial to your company?
When is the right time to utilize a chatbot, and when is it inappropriate?

In this extensive tutorial to chatbots, we will address all of these topics in addition to many others. It is my goal that by the time you reach the conclusion of this chapter, you will have a solid comprehension of what chatbots are, what they are capable of doing, how they may be of use to your company, and why and how to monitor their effectiveness.

What exactly are chatbots, and what are some of their capabilities?

A piece of software that executes tasks automatically is known as a bot. It is a piece of software that, when run on a computer, interacts with other people via the internet.

A program that has been designed and is capable of having a "conversation" or "discussion" with people is known as a chatbot. For instance, any user can pose a question to the chatbot, and it will react or carry out the corresponding action automatically.

Chatbots are computer programs that are designed to answer particular questions in a predetermined manner. Chatbots can access and utilize all of a company's resources in order to provide answers to dynamic inquiries. This means that they are not restricted to the capabilities described above.

Additionally, chatbots are able to search through multiple databases and files concurrently in order to discover answers.

Chatbots communicate with users in a manner that is analogous to that of chat platforms, such as text messages, website chat windows, and social media platforms like Instagram, Twitter, and Facebook.

Chatbots can both receive and respond to messages sent to them.

The most straightforward approach to conceptualizing chatbots is as a type of digital assistant that can be used on messaging platforms such as Facebook Messenger.

Chatbots enable businesses to communicate with clients, establish customer loyalty, automate repetitive processes, and provide outstanding customer service by drawing on the power of artificial intelligence (AI).

A chatbot's job is to engage with website visitors in the same way a real person would and to respond to any inquiries those visitors might have.

As a result, chatbots are often utilized for the purpose of automating customer support interactions for companies that receive a significant number of online questions.

You can also utilize them to make it simpler for potential customers to get prompt answers to any questions they have about your business. Chatbots are a necessary tool for streamlining client communications, as well as marketing and sales processes if you want to scale your organization.

The Advantages of Chatbots for Businesses

To be a successful business owner, you need to be as productive as you possibly can, which will allow your costs to be reduced while simultaneously increasing your profits. This is a self-evident and fundamental truth of running a business.

However, a large number of business owners do not make use of the instruments that are necessary to achieve this goal. The chatbot is a relatively new technology that is growing in popularity but is not yet utilized to its full potential by all enterprises. The replication of human language and behavior that chatbots provide offers several advantages to marketers, including the following:

1. Save Time

Time savings is one of the key advantages that your firm will enjoy as a result of implementing chatbots. If you implement chatbots on your website, they will be able to provide prompt and automatic responses to the vast majority of inquiries. Customers do not need to wait for a full day to get responses when using chatbots because the waiting time is cut down significantly.

You'll be able to serve a greater number of consumers, which will simultaneously increase your productivity and cut your operational expenses.

2. Spend less cash.

When it comes to providing quick communication to customers, using chatbots is more cost-effective than hiring a large number of customer care workers. This is because hiring more support agents involves higher costs and time.

The following are the various costs:

- Wages
- Instruction
- Facilities
- Administration

You may be able to reduce these costs by making an investment in chatbots. There are 265 billion consumer requests made each year, and corporations spend more than $1.3 trillion trying to fulfill these requests, according to recent reports.

Nevertheless, utilizing chatbots can assist you in saving up to thirty percent of your time and money. This is due to the fact that chatbots reduce the amount of time needed to respond to typical questions and can answer up to 80 percent of them.

3. Provide Automated Customer Support Around the Clock

Waiting is something that no one enjoys doing, and neither do your customers. In point of fact, 91 percent of unsatisfied customers will walk away from a brand without ever making a formal complaint.

Chatbots make it possible to interact with clients around the clock by providing instant responses to frequently asked questions. Providing outstanding customer service on a round-the-clock basis will undoubtedly have a constructive effect on the level of satisfaction and retention enjoyed by your clientele.

4. Boost Customer Engagement

It is crucial to maintain your consumers' engagement if you want to establish a successful and sustainable business. Brands that are able to engage with their customers successfully can see a 20% to 40% boost in the amount of money those customers spend.

You can elevate the degree of engagement you have with your customers to a whole new level by using chatbots. Chatbots give instant, one-on-one responses to your consumers, which is exactly what the customers desire, which in turn leads to an increase in customer happiness. By taking this method to resolve issues, you will ensure the happiness and contentment of your clients.

The real-time conversation is another feature that chatbots offer. They are the most efficient means of communicating with your customers, which results in cost savings for both parties (yours and theirs).

5. Raise the Productivity of the Team

It is anticipated that chatbots will manage 85 percent of customer support discussions without requiring any involvement from a human agent by the year 2020.

Every company will eventually move away from providing human customer support representatives in favor of automated systems, and chatbots will be an essential component of this transition.

Even though they can't totally replace human agents, they give you the ability to provide primary support that can screen a client request before it's sent to human agents.

You need to automate the processes of your sales and customer service departments in order to raise the overall productivity of your staff.

Chatbots make it possible to provide instant responses to frequently asked questions, freeing up your customer service representatives to concentrate on more critical duties that require human interaction.

6. Get better at generating leads, qualifying them, and nurturing them.

You are able to provide customized messages to clients that aid them along the "buyer's journey" by utilizing the information that is received through chatbots. This is due to the fact that you may utilize a chatbot to ask pertinent and important questions, convince the visitor, and generate leads for your business.

Chatbots ensure a smooth flow of discussion, which leads to an increase in the number of customers who make a purchase.

You can use chatbots not only to generate potential customers and notify the sales team, but you can also use them to determine the unqualified leads through identified KPIs, such as relevancy, budget, timeline, and resources. This is in addition to using chatbots to notify the sales team of potential customers and generate potential customers. Because of this, you won't have to deal with leads that require a lot of time.

Several Applications of Chatbots in the Workplace

The past ten years have seen major advancements in Artificial Intelligence (AI), and chatbots, which are one of the most beneficial outcomes of this AI progression, are among the most popular. Chatbots can assist organizations in cutting down on the amount of time it takes to respond to client questions, as well as the number of customer support representatives that are needed.

It is anticipated that the market for chatbots will reach 1.25 billion dollars by the year 2025. This is because a growing number of companies are placing a greater emphasis on the quality of their interactions with consumers.

The advantages of using chatbots go far beyond the ability to provide instant solutions to customers' questions. They are also capable of performing business duties such as gathering information about customers, organizing meetings, and lowering overhead expenses. Because of this, the size of the market for chatbots is growing at an exponential rate.

As a result, a significant number of young companies and clever brands are increasingly integrating chatbots into their day-to-day operations, interactions with customers, and sales procedures.

The following are five ways chatbots can be used in businesses:

1. Provide an Exceptional Level of Service to Your Customers

This is an excellent choice for companies that do not want their clients to:

Wait for the answer that the customer service person will give you, which will most likely be something frustrating like "Hold on while we connect you to an available customer agent."
Customers don't have time to wade through dozens of pages of frequently asked questions (FAQs), therefore you should look for answers there.

2. Make the Shopping Experience Easier to Navigate

It is enough for you to simply type in what you want into the chatbot for it to relay the information to the relevant sales staff members in order to provide a satisfying buying experience.

The phrase "I need the same product, but with metal buttons" does not need to be repeated numerous times by the customer. Additionally, the chatbot is able to remember consumer preferences, and it makes use of this information to provide repeat customers with an excellent experience.

3. Personalize Communication

Instead of showing a broad list of unimportant facts, chatbots respond with answers to the precise questions that clients have. Keep in mind that the larger the amount of attention you provide a consumer, the more likely they are to make a purchase.

This is where chatbots prove to be really useful. They allow you to send customized messages to customers and provide assistance on an individual basis, both of which will ultimately lead to an increase in your conversion rates.

4. Automate Repetitive Tasks

The majority of clients want answers to questions that are frequently asked and that are related to one another, such as "When do you open?" "In what part of the world are you?" "Do you do free deliveries?" "What is your refund and exchange policy?"

By utilizing chatbots, you won't have to keep responding the same way to the same queries every time. This will also lessen the amount of work that is required of your personnel.

5. Personal Assistant

The management of a company is a challenging endeavor. On the other hand, you can utilize chatbots as personal assistants to make your work easier to complete. For instance, you could build bots that provide clients with recommendations and hints that are pertinent to the information they are seeking.

Chatbots can provide customers with advice on trip destinations or clothing brands. And by using chatbots, you can make it simple for customers to place an order for what you have to offer.

As an illustration, MasterCard developed its own chatbot for use on Facebook Messenger. This bot streamlines the banking experience for its users by keeping track of how much money they spend monthly and displaying all of their transactions to them. Customers will find it much simpler to bank using MasterCard in this manner.

The use of bots developed by MasterCard makes it simpler for merchants to complete transactions straight within Facebook Messenger. Consumers also have the ability to place direct orders for food from restaurants such as The Cheesecake Factory, Fresh Direct, and Subway using bots.

6. Exhibit Recently Released Goods or Services

You can introduce your target audience to the most recent products or services you offer by utilizing chatbots. Because chatbots always keep up a cordial demeanor, you'll find that it's much simpler to promote your newest offerings, whether they're goods or services.

The fact that bot notifications are extremely targeted is the most beneficial aspect of these alerts. Additionally, you have the ability to select which notifications are sent to which users. Your consumers will feel appreciated and special as a result of this, and those who are unable to find products or services that are pertinent to their needs won't become frustrated.

Now that we've discussed how you may utilize chatbots to scale your business let's examine the circumstances in which you ought to make use of them and those in which you ought not.

When It Is Appropriate to Make Use of Chatbots... And Times When You Definitely Shouldn't

What methods do you use to communicate with your clients? Is the sole means for customers to get in touch with you via your website a form they can fill out, an email address, or a phone number? If that's the case, you probably need to modernize your thinking and make some adjustments.

If you want to provide a better experience for your customers, installing a chatbot on your website is a terrific method to do so.

Research indicates that over 67 percent of customers throughout the world used a chatbot in the preceding year for customer assistance. In addition, 95 percent of customers think that "customer service" will be the primary sector to benefit from chatbots.

In point of fact, 45% of customers report that chatbots are their preferred method for contacting customer service.

Therefore, in order to thrive in this new era of artificial intelligence, you will need to have experience in marketing.

Having said that, in order to derive the best value from chatbots, you need to be aware of when it is appropriate to employ them and when it is not appropriate to do so.

When Should You Make Use of Chatbots?

1. To Determine Customer Preferences and Market Tendencies, as well as Collect and Analyze Data

Chatbots provide organizations with an efficient and low-cost method of connecting with prospective customers. A chatbot is something that should be utilized by any company that conducts sales online. This is not only important for developing great relationships with your customers, but it is also important for the analytics you conduct inside.

The reason for this is that clients are far more forthcoming when speaking with bots, and the information gleaned from these exchanges can catapult your company to an entirely new level.

Chatbots are an excellent chance for businesses to collect data and determine the tendencies and requirements of their target audiences.

Consumers of today demand more than the conventional one-sided transaction; rather, they want the interaction that goes in both directions. They want to interact with and feel connected to the brands they admire the most. You'll reap the rewards of a personal, actionable dialogue through greater earnings and enhanced loyalty if you use chatbots to give a two-way connection so that customers can communicate with you in both directions.

2. To make the most fundamental of interactions easier

The ease of use that chatbots provide is the source of their effectiveness. A consumer who has a straightforward inquiry or request should be able to contact a chatbot in order to receive an instant response.

More than 53 percent of customers are likely to abandon an online purchase if they are unable to receive an immediate response to their question. Therefore, you'll be able to reduce the number of abandoned carts if you employ chatbots effectively.

For instance, a consumer who is unsure as to whether or not a particular item is currently in stock might swiftly ask a chatbot this question. Within this context, the customer and the brand will each enjoy time and labor savings.

This demonstrates a straightforward and transactional touchpoint that does not require the dexterity of a human customer care representative, who will consequently have more time on their hands to handle more in-depth concerns raised by customers.

3. Deliver Welcome Messages

Chatbots give you the ability to automate the customer service process. You can attract the attention of your clients, make them feel welcome, and put them in the mood for shopping all at the same time by integrating chatbots into your website.

4. Program Recurring Advice to Help Create Awareness of Your Brand

People take great pleasure in being motivated and continually expanding their knowledge base. Because of this, profiles that provide motivation on social media platforms like Instagram and Facebook are quite popular.

However, you shouldn't expect to make much money by simply posting motivational quotations on social media platforms like Facebook and Instagram.

Why? It's just too crowded, and everyone there is acting in exactly the same manner.
Additionally, it does not provide any assurance that the people you interact with are interested in the goods or services you offer.

You may use chatbots to communicate with your subscribers on a daily basis and provide them with pieces of information instead. Instead of sharing your content with arbitrary users on Facebook or Instagram who aren't linked with you, you may share it directly with users who are interested in it if you use chatbots.

To encourage clients to opt-in from advertisements and visit your website in order to obtain your bite-sized inspiration, you may program your planned chatbot conversation to include two button-based responses.

Because users who interact with you have consented to receive marketing communications, this type of chatbot gives you the ability to send them on a regular basis.

When It Is Not Appropriate to Use a Chatbot

In today's world, chatbots are seeing widespread use across a variety of industries, including customer service outsourcing. Chatbots have numerous advantages, but they also have some drawbacks that make them inappropriate for use in some contexts.

It is to your company's advantage to automate interactions with your clients, yet, making too much use of chatbots might result in serious issues.

Warning: Chatbots should not be used in situations that demand human interaction.

Sometimes, AI doesn't grasp it. Only people are capable of dealing with the inevitable frustrations that come with things like missing deliveries, broken products, or negative encounters with customer service.

Human customer service representatives are able to respond with empathy in emotionally charged scenarios, ensuring that their problems are addressed and resolved. Therefore, in the case that a client interacts with a chatbot in the midst of a difficult or upsetting circumstance, you should immediately transfer the customer's call to an online support representative in order to alleviate the situation and stop it from becoming worse.

Make advantage of chatbots that are able to determine when it is the appropriate time to switch topics in order to provide superior customer care.

Therefore, your chatbots should be able to recognize changes in the tone that a consumer is using or language that is emotionally laden. They ought to instantly notify a human customer support agent that it is time for them to take over at this stage in the process.

In the modern digital era, consumers' primary concern when shopping online is the safety of their personal information. In point of fact, 64 percent of customers will only shop with brands they are confident are trustworthy with their data.

Given that customers are more wary than ever about the possibility of data breaches, it is your responsibility to reassure your audience that the confidentiality of their personal information will be maintained. When it comes to the collection of sensitive information from customers, such as credit card numbers or other financial data, it is imperative that chatbots be avoided at all costs.

If you want to get the most out of your chatbots, you need to pay attention to your customers.

It will take some time before chatbots can be completely integrated into the consumer experience, just as it does with any other growing technology.

However, the most effective method for accelerating the process is to solicit input from your consumers and make use of that feedback to provide an exceptional experience for the customers.

How would you describe the journey that a customer takes with your brand? How do your customers get access to the information that you provide? What are people having difficulty with, and what are they finding to be successful strategies?

It is necessary to have a thorough understanding of these touch points before putting chatbots into action. You also need to be aware of how the use of chatbot technology will enhance the experience of your clients.

You will be able to install chatbots that offer pleasant experiences for customers if you listen to your customers and take their feedback into consideration. This will keep customers loyal to your company over the long term.

Various Forms That Chatbots Can Take Onboard

Due to their ability to simulate conversations and provide fast interactions, chatbots are quickly replacing traditional mobile applications. According to Gartner, by the year 2021, more than half of all firms will spend more money annually on the production of bots and chatbots than they do on the development of traditional mobile applications.

These days, more companies, regardless of their sector, are capitalizing on the benefits that chatbots have to offer. Chatbots not only provide round-the-clock communication for customer care, but they also provide data points that can be used to forecast client behavior.

However, the consumer base that a chatbot will serve is determined by its programming, its technology, and its nature.

Rule-based chatbots, often known as basic bots that function based on keywords, and artificial intelligence chatbots are the two primary categories that chatbots fall under.

1. Chatbots that are Governed by Rules

Rule-based chatbots were the original and are still the simplest type of bot. These are the most typical types of bots, and the vast majority of us have probably communicated with one of them before, either through a live chat feature, on social media, or on an online shopping site.

Through the use of "if/then" logic, these chatbots are able to hold a basic conversation.

The interactions that the bot will have been planned out by a human operator, such as a digital marketer, utilizing reasonable next steps and distinct call-to-action buttons.

An illustration of how rule-based chatbots function is provided below for your reference.

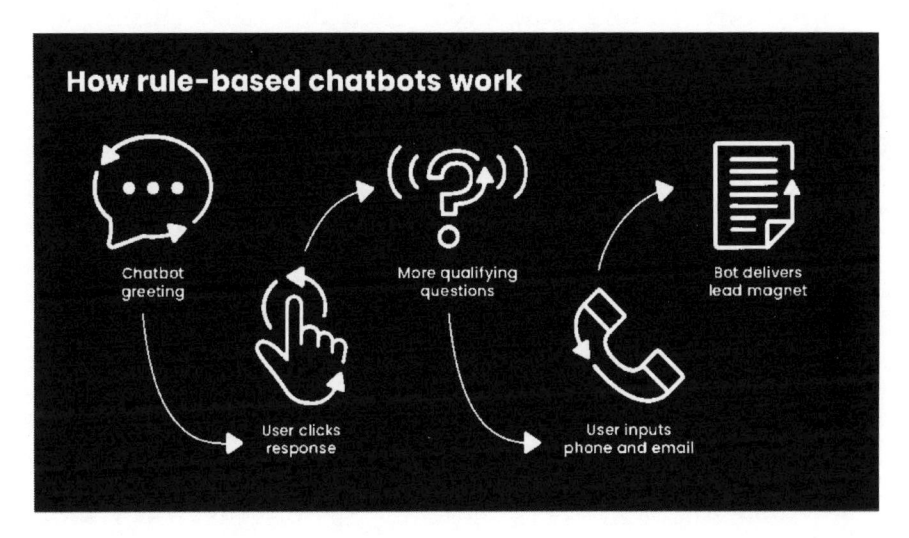

How rule-based chatbots work

Chatbot greeting → User clicks response → More qualifying questions → User inputs phone and email → Bot delivers lead magnet

As you can see, the chat begins with a welcome greeting each and every time. In addition, the site visitor needs to give permission for the chatbot to continue the conversation.

If the visitor evaluates the content as being beneficial, the bot will inquire as to whether or not they would be interested in subscribing to an email newsletter. The next step requires them to input their personal information, including their name, firm, and function in the organization.

In the event that the visitor does not choose to continue the conversation, the chatbot will inquire as to whether or not there is anything it can assist the visitor with.

Rule-based chatbots are straightforward and highly effective. Additionally, the more if/then branches that are mapped out, the better the experience that the consumer will have, as well as the less errors that will occur.

Chatbots for social media platforms

The majority of chatbots on social media are rule-based, and you can find them operating on social media platforms like Facebook and Twitter.

- Chatbots on Facebook: As of right now, there are over 300,000 different chatbots available on Facebook, making it the most popular platform for using chatbots.

- There are a lot of companies, such Sephora and Whole Foods, that use Facebook Messenger to automate their customer care, online sales, and marketing strategies.

The call-to-action buttons are the means by which Facebook chatbots connect with users.

Chatbots on Twitter Despite the fact that Twitter has a smaller selection of chatbots than other platforms, it is still a valuable medium for connecting with your audience.

For example, Etsy employs Twitter chatbots to automate their customer support interactions with customers.
As you can see, the company also makes use of CTA buttons in order to fix the issues that the customers are having.

2. Chatbots Powered by Artificial Intelligence (AI)

Rule-based chatbots are simpler in comparison to their AI-powered counterparts. These chatbots are dynamic, and they do not rely on calls to action (CTA) buttons to map out dialogues with their site visitors.

Natural language chatbots and machine learning chatbots are the two categories of AI chatbots that are now available. Smartbots is another name for these types of chatbots.
Chatbots that Understand Natural Language

Chatbots that use natural language rely on natural language processing (NLP) in order to grasp the visitor's intent and the context of the conversation, which is something that robots have difficulty doing.

We humans do not communicate in a logical manner; instead, we employ idioms, slang, and sometimes even misspell words.

And the way we express ourselves is distinct from that of machines. In order to function, machines require specifics, structures, and procedures.

NLP, on the other hand, enables machines to comprehend human language.

Instead of having to browse through buttons and menus, visitors can have a dialogue with the bot that is akin to text messaging, thanks to natural language processing (NLP). This provides a more individualized and compassionate experience overall. Chatbots that use machine learning

The functionality of these chatbots is comparable to that of natural language chatbots; however, they are designed to learn more about the visitor, remember information, and anticipate the next step in a dialogue.

Chatbots that are powered by machine learning employ artificial neural networks, which can be thought of as an artificial brain and are used to store enormous data sets. When it comes to chatbots, these sets of data are essentially previous interactions and inquiries that the chatbot can reference in order to learn new things.

In addition, machine-learning chatbots, much like their natural language counterparts, provide a more individualized experience for site visitors.

How to Measure the Performance of Chatbots and Why It's Important

The field of customer support has been completely revolutionized by chatbots. According to the projections of industry analysts, by the year 2022, banks will have automated 90 percent of their client engagements.

Consumers are pleased with chatbots; more than half of internet users are happy with them, and sixty percent of millennials use them frequently to make routine online purchases of essential goods.

On the other hand, some stories present a very different picture. For example, according to the results of a recent poll carried out by NewVoiceMedia, 46 percent of customers believe that chatbots are being utilized to block them from communicating with a real person.

And almost 43 percent of customers believe that they would rather interact with a human assistant as opposed to a chatbot.

What is the takeaway from this? You must determine how effective your chatbots are before continuing to use them. Put the following inquiries to yourself: What kind of feedback do your clients give you regarding your chatbot?

Are they content with the responses that they receive? Is this tool being utilized to its full potential? Is there a correlation between using the chatbot and making additional purchases?

It will be easier for you to find the answers to such queries if you have the appropriate key performance indicators in place.

It is essential that you measure the efficiency of your chatbot in order to track the results of utilizing it, discover any problems, and continually improve its performance.

There are five key performance indicators (KPIs) that should be monitored and analyzed to determine how well your chatbot is doing.

1. The Rate of Activation

It is necessary to verify that actual people are employing your chatbot before you can move on to evaluating its overall performance.

You may more accurately measure the amount to which clients are selecting the chatbot option by using the activation rate, which helps you identify how frequently they do so.

This key performance indicator takes into account a variety of different measures, including the overall number of users, the number of customers who open a message delivered by a chatbot, and the number of consumers who engage with the chatbot by messaging it back.

Examine new users, active users, and engaged users on a monthly basis independently while using the activation rate as a guide.

You will be able to measure the worth of your investment and, if necessary, identify new methods to employ the chatbot technology in a more engaging manner by comparing these monthly data sets.

2. Volunteer Users

You can learn more about the preferences of your consumers by doing an analysis of the number of customers who interact with a chatbot on their own smarts, rather than waiting for the chatbot to initiate a discussion with them. This demonstrates that you're branding and marketing efforts have been successful.

Volunteer users are essential; you should strive to have more of them. These are clients that have heard about your chatbot and see its worth, which is why they came to your website in the first place. These clients come in with genuine intentions, which makes them more engaged with the business.

3. The Rate of Continuation

If you can demonstrate that your consumers continue to use the automated channels you provide, it demonstrates that they regard automated engagement to be valuable.

A retention rate is the percentage of past consumers who have returned to your chatbot within a specified amount of time.

This key performance indicator will assist you in determining whether or not the current investment you have made in chatbot technology is sustainable. It will also help you determine whether or not specific components of the technology need to be refined or modified in order to provide a better experience for the customer.

It's possible that a customer's issue wasn't handled if they keep coming back to speak with your chatbot, but it's also possible that they enjoy utilizing this channel over others.

You can learn why clients keep coming back to your business by using sentiment analysis and natural language processing, such as assessing the tone of their voice.

In addition, the use of AI technology can assist you in reducing the number of friction points and the corresponding levels of consumer annoyance.

4. The Contentment of the Customers

Any company that uses chatbots for customer care needs to determine how this technology affects the level of satisfaction their clients feel. Due to the fact that messaging technology is self-serve, your customer service center has either limited or no access to the experience of end customers.

Because it isn't always obvious what the customer thinks or feels about their encounter with the chatbot, conducting an analysis of the client's level of satisfaction is obligatory.

You can accomplish this by monitoring chatbot faults and the triggers that cause misunderstanding. Alongside measurements such as Net Promoter Score (NPS), which is a loyalty indicator that analyzes the potential of your customers referring your company to others, this will identify flaws with the chatbot experience.

In most cases, the higher the customer satisfaction score those results from their interaction with a chatbot, the higher the net promoter score will be.

Also, take a look at the patterns that appear repeatedly in the client complaints that were logged by your chatbot. In addition, make a note of the recurring nature of a query and concentrate your efforts on finding a solution to the problem it reveals.

5. Response Time

Almost half of all customers have the expectation that a chatbot will provide a fast answer to their inquiries or demands. Therefore, response time is the most important indicator of how well a chatbot is performing.

It's important for a smart chatbot to be able to digest questions rapidly and deliver responses right away.

However, if the response given to the client is wrong or does not address all of their concerns, the speed with which it is given is irrelevant.

Your objective should be to provide a satisfying experience for customers by making effective use of the various tools and technology at your disposal.

If you want to provide outstanding customer service, you shouldn't let the adoption of chatbots be the end of the process, despite the inescapable fact that you will want to incorporate them into the customer experience.

It is essential to pick the appropriate KPIs to track chatbot performance and to take appropriate action based on the results wherever possible. This will allow for continuous improvement and innovation.

How to Jump Right in and Start Using Those Chatbots

The use of chatbots in online commerce is the wave of the future, and these programs are getting smarter every day. Therefore, it is prudent for the owner of any online business to make an investment right now and construct a high-quality chatbot with the goal of engaging its target market and increasing sales.

Getting started with chatbots is easy if you follow these steps.

1. Pick a System That Allows You to Create Chatbots.

When considering a chatbot for your company be sure it includes a unified inbox. What I like to call "AI-powered unified inbox" is a feature that we will use to allow you to automatically know which leads are closest to making a buying decision right now.

Then move them to the top of the pile, figuratively speaking, so you can follow up with them right away. You can follow up with them by email, telephone, chat, SMS, and even by social media messenger.

The AI-powered unified inbox is a feature that we will use to allow you to automatically know which leads are closest to making a buying decision right now and move them to the top of the pile, figuratively speaking, so you can follow up with them right away. You can follow up with them by email, telephone, chat, SMS, and even by social media messenger.

Everything all in one spot.

Check out:
AiBrandAccelerator.com

With the help of this platform, you'll have no trouble putting together chatbots for use on your website or in Facebook Messenger. In addition to this, it offers a number of fantastic integration options that are not available with any other builders. No other service offers an AI-Powered Unified Inbox."

2. Clarify Both Your Objectives and Expectations

Overloading your chatbot with too many features is the quickest way to prepare yourself for failure and set yourself up for frustration. Therefore, you shouldn't rush into trying to make your chatbot an expert in all of its duties right away.

It is preferable to construct a chatbot that is capable of mastering a single task to the best of its ability rather than having a chatbot that is capable of handling five to ten tasks just partially.

Always keep in mind that quality is more important than quantity.

3. Communicate with Your Target Audience Using the Chatbot

If you want to ensure that your customers have a pleasant experience while interacting with your company, you should directly approach them to ask for their comments and ensure that they have a positive experience overall with chatbots. When developing your chatbot, you should:

- Include a "Get Started" button that is strategically placed
- Inform your consumers how you may assist them through a welcome message
- Use buttons on your Facebook page and website
- Position your buttons effectively
- Incorporate a greeting message that is effective.

4. Create a Flowchart of the Natural Conversation

Make sure that your chatbot can hold a conversation since if it can hold a discussion, the conversation that takes place between your clients and the chatbot will be more honest. You will be able to grasp the requirements of your clients better if you do this, and you will also collect important data.

Keep in mind that the purpose of the chatbot is to provide answers to the queries posed by your consumers; therefore, it shouldn't interfere with the conversation. A good chatbot should make the dialogue easier to understand.

5. Get Your Footing by Taking Baby Steps

In addition to starting off with a limited feature set for your chatbot, the following are some additional things to bear in mind:

- When speaking with clients, try to avoid using words that are difficult to comprehend.
- Ensure that the dialogue between the bot and the user is simple and brief.
- Keep in mind that the chatbot is a symbol of your business.

You will gain the most benefit from the actions of your audience if you keep your chatbot on the basic level and keep it short. And little by little, you'll be able to construct an improved version that has a greater number of capabilities.

6. Be sure to regularly test and improve your chatbot.

You are able to broaden the functionality of your bot by developing fresh and superior iterations of it.

Because it is a tool for digital marketing, a chatbot needs to be evaluated on a regular basis and optimized in accordance with the results of such evaluations.
Because the technology behind chatbots is still relatively new, new features are being added to it on a fairly regular basis.

When you are testing your chatbots, you should:

- Determine the most effective means by which to guide your audience toward the desired result
- Adjust the settings of your chatbot in accordance with your objectives and priorities
- Determine the aspects of the chatbot that require adjustment.

7. Introduce One Feature at a Time

Your chatbot's functionality must be flawless before it can be made available to the general public. If you release a large number of features all at once to your clients, you run the risk of overwhelming them. As a result, it is essential to launch one feature at a time, at the precise moment when your audience requires them.

8. Decide what information you would like to gather and write it down.

Data collecting is made much easier with the help of chatbots. However, the data you collect will be determined to a considerable extent by the objectives you seek to accomplish.

You should begin by considering the information that you would like to obtain from your audience. Next, you should configure the conversation flow of the chatbot so that it asks the appropriate questions to obtain the information.
For example, you can:

- Ask customers about their eating, shopping, or exercising routines in order to push the appropriate offers and deals to them in the future.
- Ask about the customer's shopping preferences in order to push valuable and relevant information in your subsequent interactions with them.
- Ask for a customer's postal code if you want to know where they are located.
- Ask customers about their shopping habits in order to push valuable and relevant information in your subsequent interactions with them.

9. Maintain Current Knowledge of the Rival Companies

Because chatbots have only been around for a short while, there is still plenty of space for development. Therefore, the most effective method for getting started with chatbots is to periodically monitor the progress that your competitors are doing in this area.

In order to accomplish this, make sure that you track:

- What your competitors are doing successfully and how you can include it into your chatbot strategy
- Any unique features that your competitors utilize that you aren't familiar with in order to avoid making the same mistakes as them

Launching a straightforward, readily available, user-friendly, and efficient chatbot is now the most effective method available, as well as the most cutting-edge technique to communicate with your target audience.

And if you provide your audience a chatbot that can hold a conversation and has some personality, you can keep them interested in what you have to say.

Which Platform Should You Use for Your Chatbot?

Consider the web pages on your website that attract the most visitors who are in the target demographic for your business.

For example, if your homepage is one of the pages of your site that receives the most hits, installing a chatbot, there would be an excellent idea in order to assist site visitors in general.

In addition, if your service pages are some of the pages on your website that have the next highest impact, you should develop a chatbot for each of those sites.

And as you continue to understand what works for your company, you can continue to add new chatbots across your website that are more focused, and you can increase your skills in conversational marketing.

By utilizing chatbots, your company will have a more knowledgeable support crew that can communicate with customers via social media and your website.

This will result in less work for the customers, which will contribute to an improved customer experience.

Check out:
AiBrandAccelerator.com

Chatbots for the Purpose of Marketing

However, things take a turn for the more intriguing when you employ chatbots in your marketing efforts.

In what ways may this be useful? A good illustration of this would be making an effort to boost conversion rates the moment a visitor lands on a website.

In a normal situation, you might utilize some sales text and rely on users to discover the product listing for them by following the appropriate links and buttons on your page. This would frequently lead to confusion and dissatisfaction, and as a result, many guests would leave before they ever had a chance to look around.

The majority of websites on the internet have high bounce rates.

On the other hand, if we had a chatbot, everything might be quite different. Imagine that the instant someone visited your website, a chatbot immediately prompted them to tell it what they were looking for.

After they provided their response, the chatbot would direct them to the appropriate page where they could complete their purchase. There is no need to search the site, and there are no additional complications.

They will have revealed their 'intent' simply by telling the chatbot what they were looking for, which is another nice thing about this.

Even if a visitor does not purchase anything, they will still have given their 'intent'. The use of this kind of data can be of tremendous benefit to marketing professionals.

Additional Varieties of Chatbots

Chatbots are also capable of taking on a variety of other guises. For instance, the employment of chatbots within the Facebook message platform is becoming more and more widespread. Customers are now able to place orders at a number of eateries and fast-food locations simply by sending a message to the establishment's resident chatbot.

In addition to this, chatbots on Facebook can really reach out to prospective customers and purchasers and offer them discounts and other incentives.

Check out:

AiBrandAccelerator.com

Chapter #9

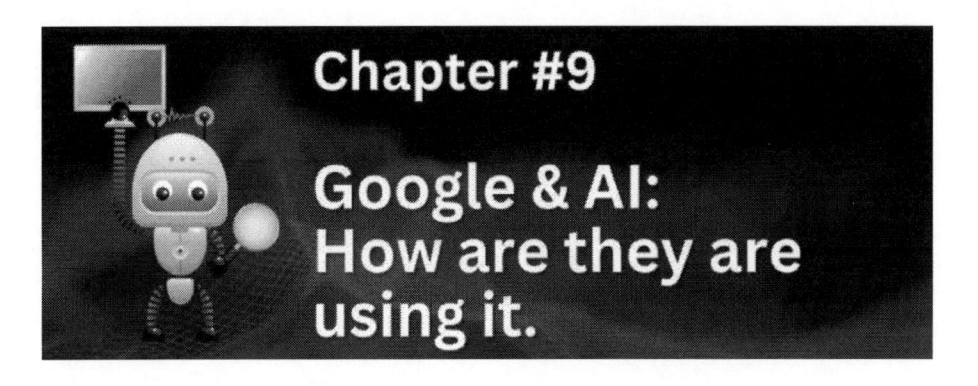

Google & AI: How are they are using it.

Google made the announcement that it was transitioning to become an AI-first firm quite some time ago. This finding may sound like worthless marketing drivel, but the reality is that it actually has HUGE potential ramifications for marketers, businesses, and search engine optimization (SEO).

To begin, could you please explain what Google means by this?

Introducing the New and Improved Google
You might think of Google as a corporation that focuses mostly on search. The first service that Google offered was a search engine, and this is the product that the majority of us still think of when we hear the name "Google."

In the past, Google's search engine did not function very similarly to artificial intelligence. Instead, the search function functioned by making an attempt to match the content of an article with the search words that were input.

Because of this, the common piece of advice given to search engine optimizers was to include a large number of key phrases within their articles. This was done so that the spiders used by Google could read the content and quickly determine whether or not it was a good match for what the user was looking for.

We are all aware that things did not go smoothly for Google as a result of this. A large number of unethical "marketers" abused the system by inserting hundreds of search phrases into each article. As a result, the content that Google would provide to the user would be distorted and unintelligible. This was caused by the "marketers'" actions.

Because of this, Google has gradually begun to behave more and more like an AI as time has gone on. Google will no longer make an effort to find precise matches for keywords anymore. Instead, Google will respond to questions that you ask by attempting to answer them. It achieves this goal by first attempting to grasp what the user is seeking as well as the context, and then by searching for responses that are relevant to the user's inquiry.

RankBrain
Through the use of machine learning, Google is able to accomplish this. Specifically, it employs a manner of natural language processing that is known as RankBrain and is a product of Google.

At the very least, RankBrain is to blame for Google's improved ability to deal with phrases and words that the search engine has never encountered before.

If RankBrain comes across a word it hasn't seen before, it can "guess" what the word might imply by taking into account the surrounding text and how the word is used in other places. Without merely matching search phrases to content in articles, this enables Google to handle unique searches that it hasn't seen before, which helps Google better serve its users.

In the process known as "distributed representation," search queries are translated into "word vectors." These are words and phrases that are comparable to one another in terms of their meaning and the context in which they are used.

After that, RankBrain will attempt to map the query into words it already recognizes or groups of phrases that are similar to one another. After that, it makes an educated guess as to what the user genuinely intends to find and what they are looking for, and it bases it results on that information. RankBrain is also capable of understanding the connections between words and how they function in tandem with one another.

At one point in time, Google did not take into consideration joining words like "the" or "and." Google has come to realize the significance of these terms and how they have an effect on the company's understanding of the user's intentions.

RankBrain, just like the most successful machine learning algorithms, makes an effort to get better over time and learn from its users. It is able to monitor which results receive the most clicks and can therefore determine when it is performing well and when it needs improvement based on this information. It is able to enhance search results for any given keyword quickly through algorithmic testing, which is helping to screen out low-quality content that seeks to cheat the system. As a result of this, it is able to improve search results.

Tensor Processing Units, or TPUs, are AI-specialized pieces of hardware that are kept in Google's data centers and are used by RankBrain to perform its functions. This is a specialized chip that has been designed to perform better than other chips when confronted with the unique difficulties of machine learning jobs.

Google's Future Goals and Objectives

It might appear that Google has diversified its operations over the past few years. It is presently in the business of manufacturing smartphones, autonomous vehicles, and software applications such as Google Lens.

However, the core of each of these endeavors is some type of artificial intelligence (AI) or machine learning. Users are given the ability to "search" the real world around them by identifying things in a scene through the usage of Google Lens, which use machine learning to accomplish this task. Artificial intelligence (AI) comes in many forms, and all of them are essential to the operation of self-driving cars.

What about Google's Pixel phones, though? It might be argued that the distribution of Google Assistant across the world is their primary priority.

This is the most important piece of information we have regarding Google's plans. Users are able to get weather forecasts, book cabs, play music, and do a great deal more with Google Assistant, which is an artificial intelligence (AI) and virtual assistant. In order to deliver helpful answers and talk in a natural manner, Google Assistant makes use of a combination of machine learning (for example, to detect human language) and artificial intelligence (AI).

Google Search and Google Assistant are very tightly connected with one another. You can ask Google Assistant questions such as "who starred in Iron Man?" and it will respond with a response that sounds very natural.

It accomplishes this goal by first applying machine learning to convert your speech into a string, then applying Google Search in order to look up useful answers (which involves machine learning in the form of RankBrain), then applying narrow AI to extract the most useful answers from the best web pages, and finally applying yet another form of narrow AI to provide the response in a natural-sounding manner (which is designed to appear like general AI.)

A significant portion of this is executed not on the device to which you are now speaking, but rather on Google's TPUs that are hosted in the cloud.

What Kind of Implications Does This Have for Marketers?

So, what does this information imply for those who work in marketing? Simply put, it implies that Google wants to be able to analyze the content of your website and pull out the information that is most relevant. It is no longer interested in you using rigid keywords, and instead wants you to get ready for a sort of search that is more voice-driven.

Artificial intelligence (AI) and machine learning are two of Google's top priorities. It forecasts that in the not-too-distant future, AI assistants will take off in popularity, and it intends for Google Assistant to be the market leader in this space. It foresees a future in which we will spend less time staring at our electronic devices and will instead obtain the information we require by inquiring about it via our mobile phones or Google Homes. These machines will understand our normal speech, and they will respond with information that is useful to us.

Check out:

AiBrandAccelerator.com

SEO and Reputation Management

Chapter #10
Preparing for Semantic Search

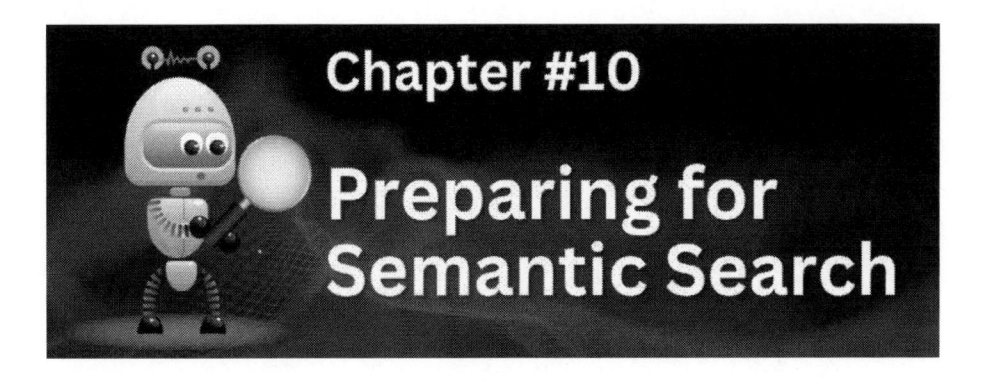

So that you know, this chapter has a lot of geeky content. Fantastic information, but in a nerdy style

Whether or not Google Assistant eventually becomes the ubiquitous tool that Google wants it to be, the fact remains that Google wants search to become increasingly more natural and human.

This goal applies whether or not Google Assistant eventually becomes the ubiquitous tool that Google wants it to be. In many different ways, it already has.

That calls for marketers and website owners to make some adjustments to the practices they already employ in their businesses. It is no longer sufficient to identify a term and repeatedly use it; instead, you need to act as though you are having a conversation with artificial intelligence. That entails a few different things to consider.

Latent Semantic Indexing, abbreviated as LSI.

If you are interested in increasing your SEO and climbing to the top of Google's search results page, one of the most significant factors to take into consideration is latent semantic indexing. It is even more crucial if you aspire to be ready for the AI-driven future that Google has in store for us. It is not just an effective idea in and of itself, but it is also an essential microcosm of the larger shifts that are taking place in SEO at this time.

It is absolutely necessary to have search engines on board if you want to attract the maximum number of people to your website or blog. Search engine optimization is a large and very important part of digital marketing, and if you want to drive the maximum number of people to your website or blog, then search engine optimization is a very important part of digital marketing.

In the past, search engine optimization (SEO) focused primarily on producing a large amount of content that was centered on a particular subject and repeatedly utilizing a predetermined number of keywords or key phrases within that content. This was done to assist Google in identifying the topic and to assist the appropriate visitors in finding your pages.

Unfortuitously, a few individuals started taking advantage of this method and started "keyword stuffing," which involves using the same keywords repeatedly to the point that they become distracting. Google recognized the need to improve its intelligence, and it did so.

To get into difficulty in today's world, you can't use the same keyword an excessive amount. So, instead of that, what does Google do? It takes into consideration the overall background as well as the primary focus of the piece.

In other words, it seeks for synonyms and related terms, which gives it the capacity to better grasp what your page is about. This ability is given to it by the fact that it looks for these things.

For example, if you had produced an article about "decision trees," then Google may possibly have been confused in the past and pulled up your site as a result when someone searched for trees. However, this is unlikely to have happened. It could have assumed that you were discussing choices to be made regarding trees!

However, it can now search for related terms such as "flow chart," which enables it to assist in making a more accurate match between the article and the reader. A method known as singular value decomposition is utilized in LSI, which originates from the field of mathematics.

This indicates that it will analyze the data in an unstructured format and search for connections between the words and ideas included within it.

LSI: A Guide to Its Management

The question now is, how can you ensure that your website is LSI optimized? To answer your question in a nutshell, no.

In spite of the fact that it is understandably enticing for SEO companies to now begin offering their LSI optimized services, the fact of the matter is that you ought to have been doing this from the beginning and without giving it any thought. That is something that the most successful web marketers, such as Andrej Ilisin, have always suggested, and it is something that Matt Cutts recommends as well.

In a nutshell, if you want to write naturally, you should make use of synonyms and discuss themes that are linked. If you don't vary your word choice, your writing will sound very repetitious. The lesson is the same as it has always been: quit second-guessing yourself and write for the reader instead! When it comes to making preparations for a more intelligent Google, this is a topic that will be revisited on multiple occasions.

If you want to make sure that Google understands what you're talking about, though, there are some additional pieces of advice that you should keep in mind.

To begin, you need to make sure that you are searching with more than one phrase. Instead of focusing on just one search word at a time, it is smart to employ a combination of multiple search terms because it improves your chances of finding what you are looking for. Because Google frequently returns search results that do not use the specific key phrase that the user looked for, it is sense to make an effort to incorporate several popular variations of the same term into your content.

In the same vein, you need to make sure that you employ a strong and broad vocabulary when discussing the topic. This contributes to a more convincing demonstration of the article's context and the subject matter it covers.

Instead of filling an article with random synonyms, consider about phrases that would frequently occur with the topic you're working with. This will make the post much more readable (such as our earlier example of flow charts.) Co-occurrence is a term for this, and it's exactly the kind of thing that machine learning algorithm' get excited about!

Data That Is Structured

Schema markups, also known as structured data and rich data, are an additional important topic that search engine optimization specialists need to think about in order to be prepared for the AI version of Google in the future.

Keep in mind that Google's goal is to make it such that Assistant can answer questions posed in natural language with responses that are helpful and that draw on knowledge obtained on the internet. In addition to producing a list of helpful search results, Google's ultimate goal is to be able to provide accurate responses to user queries. Therefore, if somebody asks how to create spaghetti bolognaise, it will merely list the components as the response.

In order for Google to accomplish this, the search engine must first be able to locate the information inside a body of text that is the most pertinent, and then it must be able to extract the precise response.

This takes the idea of RankBrain to the next level, allowing it to comprehend not only the subject matter of an article but also the function of each paragraph within that article.

The trouble is that Google's artificial intelligence isn't quite capable of doing this yet. At the very least, they are not well enough to be able to offer individuals answers that are valuable to them without occasionally incorporating replies that are absolutely absurd.

Here is where schema markups can be of use.

In essence, the purpose of schema markup is to annotate your articles and blog posts by informing Google about the nature of each component and the function it serves. You are essentially indicating that this is a list of ingredients or that this is a user rating.

The provision of what are known as "rich snippets" is facilitated as a result foofoogle.

Search results on the SERPs (Search Engine Results Pages) that provide more than simply a meta description are called rich snippets. You might, for instance, find a search result listed that also provides bullet point instructions or that includes the necessary components for the dish you want to make.

Therefore, the user does not even have to leave the website in order to view the information that they are looking for because they can view it here!

Markups: How to Make Use of Them
Markups look a lot like HTML. Take a look at the following illustration to see what I mean:
<DIV ITEMSCOPE ITEMTYPE="HTTP://SCHEMA.ORG/LOCALBUSINESS">
<A ITEMPROP="URL" HREF="HTTP://WWW.FIREFLY-

FLORAL.COM"><DIV ITEMPROP="NAME"><STRONG>THE CANDLE FACTORY</STRONG></DIV>
</A>
<DIV ITEMSCOPE ITEMTYPE="HTTP://SCHEMA.ORG/ORGANIZATION">
<SPAN ITEMPROP="TELEPHONE">888-888-8888</SPAN>
</DIV>

In essence, you are informing Google that you are referring to a local business with this (The Candle Factory). You may also utilize schema to highlight product names, authors, aggregate ratings, software application names, restaurant names, movie names, and a great many other things!

You have the option of either looking up the HTML code and implementing it on your own or using the convenient markup helper that Google provides (https://www.google.com/webmasters/markup-helper/u/0/). Either way, you can use this for your own purposes.

Simply submit the URL of the page you wish to markup in this section, and you will then be given the chance to add the appropriate tags for that page.

If you're using WordPress, there are also plugins you can utilize to accomplish the same thing.

The Positives and Negatives of Using Schema Markups
Those of you who are more knowledgeable than others may have discovered some concerning problems with schema markups. To be more specific, they actively discourage users from going to your website.

Let's imagine you own a website with recipes, and one of the articles includes instructions for making bolognaise sauce. You most likely did this in the hopes that people would look for it on Google, find your website, and then visit the page on your website to read about it.

While doing so, they may also click on a few advertisements, they may purchase a product sold by an affiliate, or may just remember your brand, which may encourage them to return to your website in the future.

If Google merely copies and distributes the most important information that you provide, however, there is little reason for users to go to your website in the first place. Because of this, there is almost no chance that they will click on your advertisements or purchase your goods. They won't be able to tell that the material originated from your website at all!

The fact that Google uses our intellectual property in this manner without paying us has angered many webmasters, business owners, and marketers. In essence, Google is using our intellectual property without paying us.

Therefore, should you completely abstain from using these features? That is not really a choice that can be made, unfortunately. Keep in mind that in order to generate rich snippets, Google makes use of markups as well. These are the more media-rich search results, including things like star ratings, photos, bullet points, and a variety of other information. These things actually make a webpage stand out in the SERPs, which in turn increases the likelihood that more people will click on the listing for that webpage.

And even if having Google read out your ingredients might not be of any advantage to you, if you don't include any markup language, it will simply grab that information from one of your rivals if you don't include it on your own website.

Because Google encourages us to use schema markups, we can assume that it will provide a slight search engine optimization (SEO) advantage to websites that make use of them. Because of all of these factors, it is imperative that you continue utilizing this method, despite the fact that you may be providing Google with free information by doing so.

In the future, if more and more people talk to their Google Assistant rather than searching the web for information, then there is a possibility that Google would need to rethink its policy: lest it face a very significant amount of pushback from content creators!

Chapter #11

SEO & Artificial Intelligence

What does this imply for the future of search engine optimization (SEO)?

Google is likely going to start paying more attention to images on websites, which is a HUGE thing that you should make sure you are ready for. One thing that you should make sure you are ready for is that Google will start paying more attention to photographs on websites.

It has been common knowledge that we should steer clear of utilizing graphics for important things like domain names. Why? As a result of the fact that Google is unable to "understand" images, there will be no positive impact on our SEO as a result of this.

However, Google does offer software that can decipher written text from a picture. This process is known as optical character recognition, and if you want to get an idea of how accurate it is, you can try aiming Google Translate at a foreign language and watching it appear in real-time in the language that you are most comfortable speaking.

If Google is capable of doing this, then it will only be a matter of time before it starts scanning the text that is contained within your photographs to determine whether or not they support the specific niche and key phrase that your website is targeting.

In the same vein, given that face recognition already plays a significant role in ensuring the safety of Facebook users, it is probably only a matter of time until Google begins to make use of this technology as well.

If you publish a blog article about Sylvester Stallone, for instance, Google might someday look not only at the content of your page but also at the photos on your website in order to determine whether or not there are any pictures of Stallone on your page!

It is possible that one day Google Images will not rely at all on the text that is surrounding the image. Instead, it may choose to base its search results only on what it sees in the image and whether or not this aligns with what you are looking for.

A significant role in the future may also be played by concerns such as the quality of the images. If Google believes that the images on your website is inappropriate or badly picked, it may decide not to promote your website to its users.

So, what exactly can you do to get ready for it? For the time being, the usage of markup language and/or file names and alt tags is the item that comes the closest to interacting with Google through the use of images. If you use alt tags to explain photos, you may assist Google in understanding what the images are trying to convey, and it will be easier for it to determine whether or not your website is relevant to a specific user.

In the meantime, check to see that all of the imagery you are using is both pertinent and of high quality.

Chapter #12

Advertising / ROAS

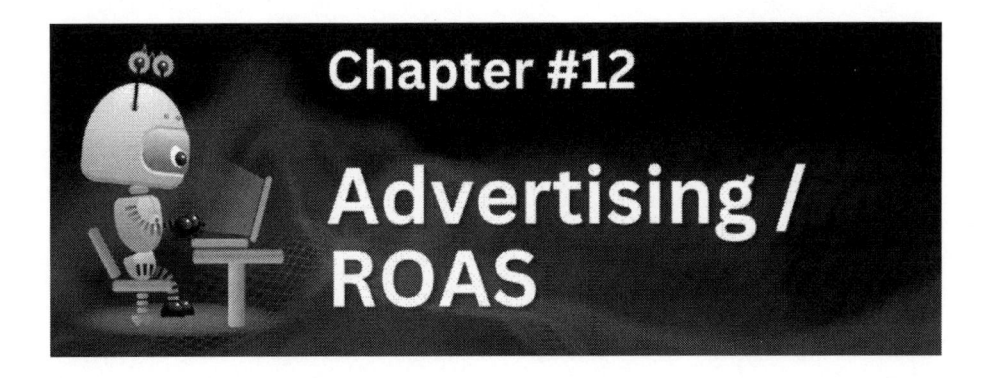

Learning by machine is, at its heart, an exercise in evolution. Increasing the amount of data that is collected until it is capable of producing more reliable inferences is the goal here. Although it's possible that the system's first face detection in photos will be inaccurate, over time it will improve and learn to the point where it will be more accurate than a person.

Imagine being able to put that power to use in the advertising industry. Imagine for a moment that you had the ability to display the most relevant adverts to the most relevant individuals at the most relevant times.

Imagine for a moment that your advertising campaign somehow "evolved" so that it became more and more targeted, resulting in an ever-increasing number of viewers clicking on the commercials and purchasing your goods.

If you ran the campaign for a longer period of time, not only would your revenues rise, but you would also reduce the amount of money you spent on advertisements that were ineffective.

That is exactly how the process of programmatic advertising works, and you can get started utilizing it right away!

What exactly is meant by the term programmatic advertising?

Using a bidding system that allows them to compete with other advertisers for impressions, programmatic advertising campaigns enable marketers to buy native ads on a variety of publishers' websites while using smart algorithms to ensure that they are targeting the right viewers at the right times. This is all accomplished while staying within budget, thanks to the fact that they are able to target the right viewers at the right times.

In a nutshell, these campaigns provide the control, adaptability, and precision that you would get with a pay-per-click (PPC) campaign while at the same time giving the precision and quality that you would receive from native advertising (such as banner ads). The end result is that advertisements will appear on the websites of carefully chosen publishers, but only when and if such advertisements are likely to produce the best outcomes.

Identifying your company's ideal consumers and determining where they are most likely to be found online can both be accomplished with the use of a complicated algorithm that is used in programmatic advertising.

After that, it will display the advertisements in those locations and then use a learning process so that rather than going from one publisher to another talking pricing, you can let a "bot" do all of the work for you.

However, this does ensure that you won't waste money on an ad position that no one looks at, which is perhaps the most essential benefit. Your advertisements will be selected and improved by an algorithm, and as a consequence, they will receive greater CTRs from the customers who are most likely to be interested in them.

RTB

When compared to PPC advertising or simply purchasing a banner ad on your preferred news website, programmatic purchasing is distinguished in the following way. The ability to employ RTB, often known as "Real Time Bidding," provides you with even greater control in the meanwhile.

You will be entered into a bidding war automatically each time a page loads, and the amount of the war will be determined by the budget you have set beforehand. This is what RTB fundamentally means.

Your advertisements will be able to compete with those of other advertisers across a wide variety of websites, each of which is tailored to the particular demographics and context that you have selected through the use of these bidding wars.

In other words, you will specify that you wish to target sports websites that are aimed at males in their 20s to 40s, and from that point on, your advertisements will appear across a selection of those websites (which you can still curate in some instances if you so desire) based on the outcome of each individual bid. This enables you to target your audience across a variety of different websites while minimizing the amount of money you need to spend in order to do so.

Direct purchase, on the other hand, refers to the practice of placing a large order for impressions from a particular website or websites, such as ESPN. You will still be able to restrict your impressions by a variety of parameters like location or browser, but in essence, you will be targeting a certain site and securing a space on that particular spot.

In practice, direct buying is more comparable to advertising with a banner ad, although real-time bidding (RTB) is somewhat more analogous to the pay-per-click (PPC) approach, in which you place bids for spots on a variety of websites (while still having a little more control).

The answer to the question of what will be most successful for you is going to be determined by a number of different things. For instance, your financial plan will come into play as a result of the fact that direct purchase is typically more expensive (due to the fact that there won't be as many possibilities for lower CPIs to arise).

You may detect which websites are functioning best for you, at which times, and for which viewers, and then further adjust your strategy in accordance with that information. Real-time bidding (RTB) allows you more freedom, more data, and more control. It is important to keep this in mind.

If, on the other hand, you place a bid that is too low when employing RTB, you run the danger of your advertisements never displaying at all. Direct buys, on the other hand, "ensure" both your ad space and the fact that you will eventually be certain to receive a particular number of impressions.

This stands in stark contrast to the aforementioned direct buys. This is helpful for a corporation that has clear goals and a set timetable to accomplish them. In the same vein, if you use direct buying, you will have a greater degree of control over the placement of your advertisements and will be able to establish a more intimate connection between your brand and that of the publisher.

Therefore, different strategies will be effective for various types of marketers and for various kinds of goals. Your task is to hand, determine which works best for you, and the best way to do so may very well be to dip your toe in the water and test them out for yourself. Your job is to decide which works best for you.

How to Achieve Greater Success with Automated or Programmatic Purchasing

Programmatic advertising has shot to the forefront of the online marketing industry in a very short amount of time and has emerged as an essential new tool for any company that aspires to communicate with a larger customer base.

However, even the most advanced programming tools are only as useful as the people who control them. With that in mind, before you go too far ahead of yourself, it is important to examine the following four essential guidelines to assure your success.

Don't Ignore the Part That Involves Creativity

If you haven't put any effort into making your advertising creative, they won't be successful no matter how well-targeted they are or how well thought out your campaign is in terms of exposure.

If you haven't put any effort into making your commercials creative, they won't succeed. Create effective commercials by first designing them, then testing them to determine which designs perform the best. In a similar vein, you should think about the identity of your brand and how you can strengthen it even through advertisements that aren't clicked on. Find a partner in the programming who can assist you with this facet of the project.

Take into account both the audience and the context.

Before deciding which publications to collaborate with, you should first consider the audience that each one draws as well as the context in which they operate. A website that writes about issues that are similar to yours and that targets the exact same demographic as you are would be a great partner for your business.

In some instances, though, you won't be able to find both, and as a result, you'll have to choose publications that offer the optimal level of both variety and coherence. Also, resist the urge to ignore the context of the event, because research has shown that the same individual is much more likely to click on an ad for golf equipment when they are on a golfing website as opposed to a news site.

This is something that you should keep in mind. To get more specific, someone who wants a wedding dress is only going to want that wedding dress during a specific time in their life, and this further emphasizes how important it is to take into account the context of one's desires.

Be prepared to spend money right off the bat.

The benefit of using programmatic advertising is that it enables you to directly manage your spending in real-time, which guarantees that you will receive the most exposure no matter how much money you spend. However, it is highly recommended that you begin with a bigger spending limit than you want to continue with.

This will help you to more quickly determine what works and what does not work for you, which will save you time and money in the long run.

Keep in mind that you want more data, which means you want more clicks on your links. You will get closer and closer to the optimal set-up for your campaign as you make adjustments in response to stats and ROI, but if you don't spend the money upfront, you won't be able to tell if your campaign is working because you won't win enough bids to determine whether or not your campaign is successful. Spending a bit more now will save you a lot more money in the long run as you get into your routine and find your rhythm.

Check to See That Your Ads Are Appropriate

The disadvantage of running an automated advertising campaign is that you run the risk of losing the "personal touch." The "personal touch" refers to the benefits that come from working with a publisher to develop an advertising campaign that matches the tone and appearance of their overall site and that they will help to promote throughout their content. This "personal touch" can be lost if you run an automated advertising campaign.

Unfortunately, native advertising is tough to scale, which is one of the reasons why there is such a high need for autonomous platforms.

This is something you need to think about if you want to have any level of success with programmatic advertising. Your advertisement is being displayed to the appropriate individuals, on the appropriate devices, and in the appropriate settings.

But does it have the necessary qualifications to do the job? This advertisement ought to have the appearance of a native advertisement in the same manner that a banner advertisement would.

One method for accomplishing this goal is to design advertisements that are adaptable enough to fit into a variety of "environments." Another option is to find a platform that gives you the ability to choose the companies with whom you want to collaborate, and then pick the ones that are already most closely aligned with your objectives and aesthetic preferences.

Check out:
AiBrandAccelerator.com

Chapter #13: Email Marketing

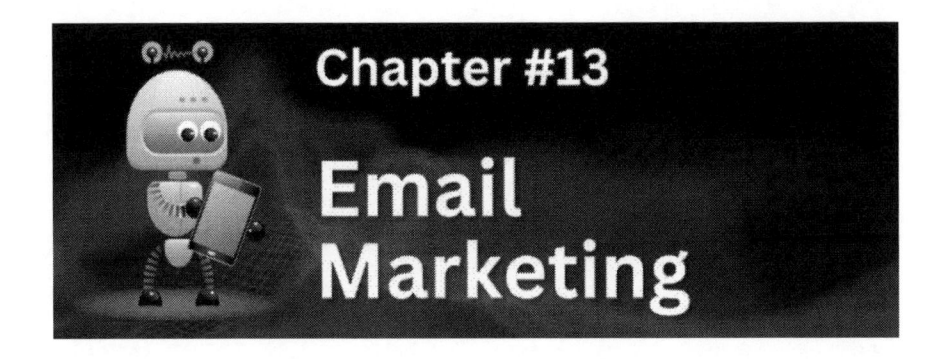

Gaining traffic is important, but controlling that traffic is even more crucial for online success.

Why does that matter? It implies that you must be able to choose, at any time, which of your visitors you want to speak with. It implies that you must comprehend your customers and be aware of their thoughts, feelings, and areas of interest at all times.

In order to sell things or entice people to join your mailing list, you must be aware of the best times to strike. This is a recurring theme in machine learning and artificial intelligence. The same is true for email marketing.

By creating a mailing list and then segmenting it, you can accomplish all of this.

Let's first review the fundamentals of email marketing for those who are unfamiliar.

Of course, email marketing refers to the practice of marketing by email. In other words, you'll be creating a large list or a collection of emails, and you'll do it by requesting contact information from site visitors as soon as they arrive at your home page.

An autoresponder is thus necessary as a result. You can use an autoresponder to make email forms and then to handle every contact on your list.

People can enter their information into the form on your page, and the autoresponder will send all of your emails on your behalf.

Check out:
AiBrandAccelerator.com

The benefit of this should be readily clear.

It's difficult and unlikely that many of your emails would get delivered if you tried to send them all manually using Gmail or another online client. Longer lists would need you to send several distinct emails and manually handle any requests for subscription or unsubscription.

All of it is handled by an autoresponder, so all you have to do is compose one email and hit "send." However, another advantage of using an autoresponder is that it can gather data for you and use that data for a variety of purposes.

An autoresponder, for instance, can display information such as the proportion of subscribers who really read your emails. If the subject lines of your emails aren't successfully enticing recipients to read them, you can pinpoint the issue and work to find a remedy.

All of a sudden, machine learning and a data-driven strategy is being used! Then, you can get a list of all the visitors who did read a particular message. Or decide to view every single one that didn't. You can sort your list according to various criteria and view the open rate for certain specific visitors.

Another useful benefit of having an autoresponder is that you can group your visitors using the additional information you can collect through the form that is integrated on your page.

Do you only want to message the men? Try it out. Do you

only want to contact those above 30? The same applies to you. Or how about having many mailing lists for various brands or even various products? You can complete all of this with only one autoresponder.

Of course, this level of command and automation gives marketers a plethora of options when it comes to AI and machine learning.

Warming of leads and email segmentation

The ability to use this data to pick and select who receives your communications gives this information its actual power. You could specify, for instance, that you only want to send emails to persons who fit into certain categories.

Sending emails depending on lead warming, lead retention, and engagement is what we're interested in initially.

Anyone who has expressed interest in making a purchase from you is considered a lead. That implies that anyone who has subscribed to your mailing list can be regarded as a lead as they have already shown interest by doing so.

However, anybody who sees your website or requests your card is likewise a lead. This is a "cold" lead, as opposed to a "warm" lead, which is someone who really provides you with their contact information.

The more interest a lead expresses in what you do and what you sell, the warmer the lead becomes. Additionally, a lead is more likely to make a purchase from you if they are warm.

In fact, turning ice-cold leads into warm leads and eventually paying customers is the real and most practical benefit of having a mailing list in the first place.

This is what I usually compare to requesting someone's phone number. Someone would probably just tell you to leave if you approached them in a club and asked for their phone number.

When they don't know anything about you and haven't expressed any interest in you, why would they offer you their phone number?

You must first converse with them and give them a chance to get to know you. They are a cold lead if they smile while looking at you. A warm lead is someone who responds to your smart chat and gives you, their name. They are a hot lead if they have kissed you or allowed you to buy them a drink. When they become desirable, you might ask for their phone number.

Timing is everything in this. If you time this wrong, they won't give you their phone number since you haven't set up the situation.

Internet marketing is exactly the same way. They won't buy your stuff if you tell someone who views your website to do so immediately now. the reason why? They have no reason to believe you now. You haven't given them any personal information. They don't have a lot of product knowledge.

However, after a few blog posts, ask them for their email and you can gradually start to develop involvement. This is the time when you truly wow them with your knowledge and facts. You engage them in light entertainment while letting them get to know you.

If they don't even open your emails, it's the same as them ignoring you. That's like the club patron who doesn't laugh at your jokes and keeps turning her or his head. Right now, if you try to sell to them, you turn into spam. And you're eliminated.

They also never come back to your website.

However, if they open your emails, you know you have a chance. That allows you to inform them of your products in greater detail and pique their interest in your next product launch. Your chances of success increase if they continue to open your emails throughout that time. There is a far greater likelihood that they will buy from you if you try to sell to them right away.

You can determine which of your visitors are actually reading your emails, clicking your links, and scrolling to the bottom using email segmentation, which allows you to do just that.

It is actually possible to determine which of those visitors has visited your website and looked at your merchandise utilizing cookies. You can discover who has looked at your products and considered purchasing them.

Combining machine learning with email segmentation

If you've been following along closely, you might have already realized where this is going. Recall how we stated you could use predictive analytics to more accurately rate leads when we talked about big data?

The future of autoresponders may get pretty interesting at this point. Imagine if your autoresponder could analyze massive amounts of data to find trends in addition to audience segmentation, open rates, and engagement.

What if, in other words, your autoresponder tracked every customer who made a purchase from you and determined what steps they typically took first? This would make it easier for the machine learning system to recognize when a user is acting in a way that suggests they are ready to make a purchase and send them a message designed to encourage that action!

This might be paired with informed recommendations to increase the possibility that they'll make additional purchases.

It won't be long before more of us have access to the same level of precision since several major brands are already using it.

Advice for Marketers Right Now

You also need to make sure that people are joining your mailing list in the first place for any of it to function. Again, this will aid in our readiness for a world powered by AI. There are various methods you can use to support this.

First, be sure to display your mailing list as much as you can. That should, at the very least, result in the display of your mailing list at the end of your entries. To ensure that your list is displayed on every page of your website, you can also put this in the sidebars at the same time.

Make sure to call attention to it as another piece of advice. A common error is for people to start their email list and then merely "hope" that people will read it. It's much more beneficial to mention it on occasion and to justify why it's a worthwhile opportunity and why people should be eager to sign up in your posts.

But here's the thing: You should always be truthful.
A mailing list's goal is not to expand as much as possible. Instead, the objective is to increase its size as much as possible using only extremely focused visitors.

You will just annoy them and, in essence, be spamming them if your visitors have no interest in what you're selling through your list.

Check out:
AiBrandAccelerator.com

Chapter #14
Case Studies

10 Top Brands using AI for years

Some of the most successful brands in the world are aware of something that you are not. They are cognizant of the fact that artificial intelligence is more than simply a buzzword.

It is actual technology that is generating actual marketing benefits for their businesses. There is a lot of hyperbole surrounding AI; that much is true.

However, because of this, it is extremely important for marketers and leaders in business to investigate how actual organizations are utilizing genuine tools to produce revenue.

When you do, a compelling picture will come into focus, which is as follows:

The most successful companies in every sector are turning to AI to increase their sales, deliver remarkable customer experiences at scale, and modernize their business procedures. Over 750 AI-powered startups have received funding of more than $4 billion.

Olay
Wouldn't it be great if, in just two years, you could treble the conversion rate at your company?

In any case, with the assistance of artificial intelligence, it is not out of the question at all; just ask Olay.

The year 2016 saw the beginning of artificial intelligence deployment at the Procter & Gamble corporation with the introduction of the Olay Skin Advisor.

The user submits a selfie to the web tool, and the tool then provides a report that includes an accurate skin-age assessment as well as advice for care.

The selfies are analyzed by the AI-powered engine in the background, and the results are used to recommend specific products and care routines to users.

Olay has been able to not only double its conversion rate but also boost its average cart size (it climbed by 40 percent in China alone) and cut its bounce rate by two-thirds ever since it introduced Skin Advisor.

Cars.com
With the use of artificial intelligence (AI), Cars.com has developed a platform that makes it simpler to find your next vehicle. The artificial intelligence application makes car suggestions for consumers by employing an algorithm that is based on their preferences for machine learning.

Cars.com employs sentiment analysis to deliver up to 20 recommendations once the user has completed a survey that provides the machine with feedback on 15 different lifestyle choices.

When compared to the traditional search function of the organization, the matchmaking model's pilot resulted to a 752% increase in profile creation, an 87% rise in return visits, a 225% jump in email leads, and two times more page views per visitor than the traditional search function.

This is not the first time that Cars.com has dabbled in the field of artificial intelligence.

In April, the website launched a function known as "Hot Car," which makes use of machine learning to determine which automobiles are most likely to be purchased in a short amount of time.

UPS

UPS is the clear front-runner when it comes to artificial intelligence (AI) implementation in big brands.

In point of fact, the majority of the company's operations are driven by AI at this point. Customers can identify UPS locations, track their shipments, and get shipping costs with the help of a chatbot that is powered by artificial intelligence (AI).

Customers are able to have natural conversations with the bot through platforms such as Facebook Messenger, Skype, Amazon Alexa, and the mobile app for UPS.

In addition to this, it uses ORION, a highly advanced artificial intelligence platform, to plan and optimize the routes that UPS drivers use.

The vehicles used by UPS are outfitted with computer systems that can record logistical data. After that, AI algorithms and deep learning are used to the data in order to improve routes and shave off millions of annual miles from UPS's routes.

That will result in significant cost reductions for a business that already invests a significant amount of money each year in gasoline and employee wages. In addition to this benefit, it boosts both the speed and dependability of UPS delivery.

Last but not least, the EDGE initiative at UPS is a collection of dozens of projects that are being carried out across the whole company to make use of the enormous amounts of data that are being gathered by the company from its many operations.

AI is used to examine this data in order to draw conclusions about a variety of topics, including when vehicles should be washed and how trucks should be loaded.

According to an article published in Technology Review, "once the program is completely deployed, the corporation expects to save between $200 and $300 million annually."

Fridays at TGI
Just by applying artificial intelligence, the restaurant business TGI Fridays was able to increase its off-premise sales by 50 percent, bringing in an additional $150 million in income.

According to VentureBeat, rather than spending tens of thousands of dollars developing a custom artificial intelligence system tailored exclusively for TGI Fridays, chief experience officer Sherif Mityas outsourced the work to three primary software tools.

Amperity, a tool that has been around for about nine months, is being utilized to piece together all of TGI Fridays' data. Email interaction, in-store receipts, information from loyalty programs, app activity, and a variety of other factors are taken into consideration. After that, it sends customized offers to customers by utilizing techniques such as decision-tree branching that are associated with machine learning.

TGI Fridays use the chatbot startup Conversable to handle all of its message platforms, including Facebook, Twitter, Amazon, and Alexa. Instead of answering with alternatives A, B, and C like other chatbots, this one-use natural language processing (NLP) to comprehend what the consumer is asking and provides a new answer every time.

Last but not least, TGI Fridays collaborated with Hypergiant to develop a Virtual Bartender who goes by the moniker Flanagan.

It has produced over 300 unique flavor profiles so far, all of which are based on the specific moods, preferences, and patterns of behavior of bar patrons.

Virgin Holidays
The sale of vacation experiences by Virgin Holidays brings in hundreds of millions of dollars annually. Because a significant portion of its sales is conducted by email, even a moderate increase in the number of engagements and conversions would be worth a fortune.

When you employ something like artificial intelligence, it turns out that amassing a fortune is a lot simpler. To accomplish this, Virgin Holidays utilized an artificial intelligence application known as Phrasee.

Phrasee employs artificial intelligence to write the subject lines of email messages automatically. These subject lines read like they were written by humans, yet they perform significantly better than those.

By utilizing the tool, Virgin Holidays was able to increase its open rates by 2%, which resulted in an increase of millions of dollars in new revenue. In addition, the process of writing subject lines now only takes a few minutes, it used to take several weeks. This allows the brand's marketers to focus their efforts on more important projects.

Acrolinx, an artificial intelligence platform, uses techniques such as machine learning and natural language processing (NLP) to enhance the content of some of the most well-known companies in the world, including Boeing, Caterpillar, and Nestle.

Acrolinx is used by a wide variety of companies, including Boeing, Caterpillar, and Nestle, to improve the quality of their content by employing AI-powered scoring and suggestions. Acrolinx also monitors a company's content to see whether or not it complies with its brand and internal guidelines.

The artificial intelligence platform utilized by the company makes use of a one-of-a-kind linguistic analytics engine to "read" all of the information that is connected to each of these companies and then offers immediate suggestions on how to improve it. In turn, this information is used to inform how these brands develop content that performs well.

Acrolinx does more than only supply companies like Boeing, Caterpillar, and Nestle with precise predictive analytics on the effectiveness of their content; the company also guides content contributors on how to maintain each company's content so that it remains on-brand and on-target.

L'Oreal
L'Oréal, one of the leading cosmetics firms in the world, has a responsibility to be present wherever its clients may be.

This also applies to the voice search.

In order to get the highest possible ranking in voice searches, the company decided to utilize BrightEdge, an SEO and content platform that is powered by AI.

After all, voice search only provides one audible result, so it's a case of winner-take-all in this particular competition.

L'Oréal made use of BrightEdge's artificial intelligence to identify searches and phrases for which the company was in a position to claim the top result, and then they focused their SEO efforts on achieving that goal.

Carlos Spallarossa, head of SEO for L'Oréal, said in an interview with BrightEdge that "it has become the cornerstone of our content strategy."

Overstock
Every single day, Overstock moves a significant quantity of products through the use of email marketing.

You could therefore conclude that it was a rather significant problem when they experienced a dip in their email delivery rates.

In point of fact, every email that wasn't delivered by Overstock was a lost opportunity to generate income.

In order to diagnose their deliverability challenges, the organization turned to Return Path, an email platform powered by artificial intelligence.

Overstock's inbox placement rates "averaged 98 percent and often surpassed 100 percent at their most critical domains" after the company worked with the platform and professionals from Return Path for several months.

What is the result? Profit increases as a result of using AI.

T-Mobile
When your company has more than 3,500 brick-and-mortar locations and millions of customers visit those locations annually, you need to ensure that your brand is visible in the appropriate online searches.

T-Mobile was responsible for ensuring that its stores were visible to customers who conducted internet searches for them and that the location information associated with each store was correct.

Implementing this strategy on a larger scale seems to call for significant investments of both time and resources.

Therefore, the business decided to use Yext, a platform for digital knowledge management that provides businesses with control over the brand experiences that are presented across maps, applications, search engines, voice assistants, and other intelligent services that make use of AI to surface search results.

In just the first year, the platform that Yext offers was able to supply more than 45 million accurate listings in the results of search queries. Additionally, Yext was able to assist T-Mobile in removing duplicate location data from Google, which was a source of confusion.

As a consequence, T-visibility Mobile's in local search has been steadily improving, and the company's brand perception and loyalty have seen a significant increase as a result.

Check out:
AiBrandAccelerator.com

Chapter #15
How to Future Proof Your Marketing

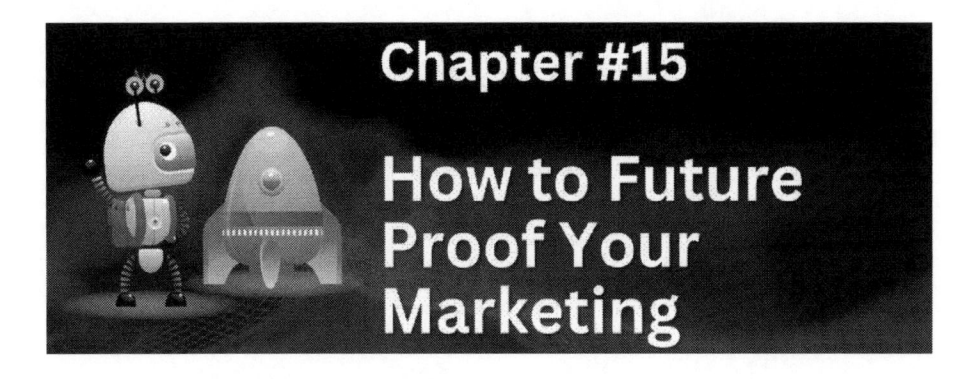

Throughout the course of this book, we have covered a wide range of topics pertaining to the application of AI and machine learning within the field of digital marketing.

The purpose of everything that has been discussed up until this point has been to assist you in becoming more prepared for the future. You are aware that you should immediately begin to collect as much data as is humanly feasible, that you ought to incorporate schema markups into your website, that you ought to make use of LSI, and that you might gain anything from a chatbot...

But it's highly likely that a lot of these things are going to shift quite a bit more before the new development arrives on the scene, and we can't really predict how its influence will be felt at this point.

The significance of artificial intelligence (AI) is difficult to understate in light of the enormous waves currently moving across online marketing.

Consider, for example, what will take place once AI that is capable of producing content of a high standard is widely adopted and made accessible for sale. This technology already exists - artificial intelligence that can write nearly as well as a human – but when it is let to run wild on the web, it has the potential to flood the internet with sufficient fresh information to double or triple its size in a couple of days.

How can we tell the difference between something that was written by a person and something that wasn't?

What about when AI is able to make visuals that look completely real?

Deep fakes have already demonstrated their power; the question now is how we can differentiate between genuine and fake information.

Because we do not know how any of these potential outcomes will play out, we are unable to adequately prepare for them. Therefore, for the time being, it is advisable to concentrate on the things that we already know. And more specifically, as a marketer, this means concentrating on Google's shift toward natural language processing and interactions that are more similar to those between humans.

It also indicates that Google will continue to improve in terms of its intelligence. Google used to check for keyword matches, but now it genuinely understands what a website is and can use many more indicators to determine whether or not a website is of high or low quality and whether or not it delivers on what it promises to do.

As a matter of fact, Google probably has the potential to become the most powerful artificial intelligence on the planet. This is because Google has access to an enormous quantity of information, and the corporation pours enormous resources into developing its AI. Because of this, attempting to "game" the system or deceive Google will become ever more challenging.

What is our best course of action, then? Create content of the highest possible quality. Writing for Google and writing for the reader will come to mean roughly the same thing as Google's artificial intelligence improves, and it becomes more human.

It is time for us to start concentrating on producing content of high quality and on giving actual value to our audience.

One of the most important things to keep in mind about Google is that the company puts its users' needs first. Who exactly are its clients? The users access it in order to obtain knowledge and enjoy themselves.

Because Google wants people to continue using its search engine, the company needs to make sure that it always displays just the information that is both the most pertinent and the most fascinating.

If you focus on producing high-quality material for your audience, then the goals that you have for your site and those that Google has for its site will be compatible. Therefore, every time it grows a little bit smarter, that will work to your advantage rather than being something that you need to worry about.

As Google continues to improve its artificial intelligence, it will discover additional methods for determining which content has the highest quality. If you concentrate on providing that, then Google will look for other ways to link you up with the people who are interested in what you have to say.

If you combine this with more data collecting and a marketing strategy that is more data-driven in general, you will be prepared for the changes that are coming to the sector in the future.

Make sure you have everything you need to make your artificial intelligence system function properly before you make any investments in it.

Find out what you're going to need, what kind of specialists you might need to bring on board, and what kind of additional charges might show up later on.

When looking to implement AI into your company, it is not always necessary to engage a data scientist. There are hundreds of companies that are working on developing AI solutions that are simple to use for solopreneurs and small businesses.

For instance, using the tools provided by Legal Robot can assist you in developing legal documents and contracts that are understandable and in compliance with applicable regulations. Additionally, using an application powered by AI, such as Grammarly, can provide you with writing that is consistent and of high quality.

A growing number of companies are already providing customer care via chatbots, and these can be predesigned for your company.

Since they were initially launched, chatbots have gone a long way. They have improved in areas such as natural language processing, which has made them even more effective and reduced wait times for human customer support representatives.

You, as an entrepreneur, have a ton of options to set yourself apart from the other businesses in your industry thanks to the practically endless applications for artificial intelligence.

If your business would like to start leveraging AI check out:

Check out:
AiBrandAccelerator.com

Chapter #16
What is ChatGPT?

What is Chat GPT and Why Should We Care?

Who did the work?

The new artificial intelligence is a chatbot that was developed by the independent research group OpenAI foundation, which was founded by Elon Musk.

Late in 2015, Musk and several other investors from Silicon Valley, including the technology venture capitalist Sam Altman, co-founded the startup. Musk stated at the time that the research center would "advance digital intelligence in a way that is most likely to benefit humanity." This was according to a blog post written at the time.

Since then, the CEO of Twitter has resigned from the board of directors and has distanced himself from the company. On Sunday, he tweeted that he had put a halt to OpenAI's access to the platform's database for "training" when he "discovered" that OpenAI was doing so.

According to what he had to say, there is a "need to grasp more about governance structure [and] revenue strategies going forward." "OpenAI was first developed as a non-profit, open-source project. Neither of those things is still the case."

How does it work?

The system is capable of providing information and responding to questions using a conversational user interface. It was trained using artificial intelligence and machine learning.

The artificial intelligence has had its training done on a massive amount of text gathered from the internet.

According to OpenAI, the new AI was developed with an emphasis on how easy it is to use. "The dialogue format makes it possible for ChatGPT to answer follow-up questions, admit its mistakes, challenge incorrect premises, and reject inappropriate requests," the research body said in a statement last week. "The dialogue format makes it possible for ChatGPT to answer follow-up questions, admit its mistakes, challenge incorrect premises, and reject inappropriate requests."

What applications does it have?

Early adopters of the technology have referred to it as an alternative to Google due to the fact that it is able to provide descriptions, answers, and solutions to complex questions. These answers and solutions include ways to write code, as well as ways to solve layout problems and optimization queries.

Applications in the real world might include things like generating content for websites, responding to questions from customers, making suggestions, and even building automated chatbots.

The chief executive officer of OpenAI, Sam Altman, described the system as "an early demo of what's conceivable." "Soon, you will be able to make use of helpful assistants that can converse with you, respond to your inquiries, and offer suggestions.

In the future, you will be able to have something that operates independently and completes things on your behalf. You will eventually be able to have something that explores the world and finds new information specifically for you.

Would ChatGPT be able to take the role of humans?

It has been hypothesized that careers that are dependent on the production of content may become extinct in the future. These careers include anything from playwrights and professors to programmers and journalists.

Academics have generated responses to exam questions that they say would result in full marks if submitted by an undergraduate, and programmers have used the tool to solve coding challenges in obscure programming languages in a matter of seconds. These developments have taken place in the days since it was made available to the public.

The capability of the technology to generate written content that is eerily similar to that produced by humans has led to speculation that it could one day replace journalists.

However, in its current state, the chatbot does not have the nuance, critical thinking skills, or ethical decision-making capacity that are necessary for effective journalism. These abilities are vital.

The existing version of its knowledge base will be retired in 2021, which would render certain inquiries and searches obsolete.

The business admits that ChatGPT is capable of providing "plausible-sounding but incorrect or nonsensical answers." It can also provide answers that are completely false and pass off erroneous information as fact.

According to OpenAI, it will be difficult to solve this problem because the data they use to train the model do not contain any reliable sources of information, and supervised training can also lead to inaccurate results "because the ideal answer depends on what the model knows, rather than what the human demonstrator knows."

If you are anything like me, you will eventually develop a strong dislike for whatever it is that everyone else seems to be talking about. Simply because of this. Before giving it the benefit of the doubt.

ChatGPT is now available. I had a strong negative reaction to it while not having a good understanding of what it was. Therefore, in order to avoid falling once again into that lazy trap of disliking the thing that everyone else seems to be talking about, I decided to conduct my own research on the topic. You might compare it to something you'd find online.

If I hadn't been paying attention, I would have been finding more and more tweets like this one. And I would have kept rolling my eyes and attempting to discover things that truly intrigued me, such as films of divers interacting with tiger sharks in the water.

Something That Can't Be Ignored

It seems that this ChatGPT thing is a rather significant development for some reason. Everyone on social media who has an opinion and claims to have had a conversation with the trending new chatbot, ChatGPT, thinks that ChatGPT is about to replace everything from Google search to higher education.

To put it simply, it's an AI chatbot. OpenAI was responsible for the development of ChatGPT, which was based on the GPT-3.5 model produced by the AI research lab. The chatbot is programmed to hold conversational exchanges.

Also, if you ask it to, it will supposedly compose an article for you to submit.

A simple interpretation of this situation is that anyone who earns money from college students by ghostwriting their essays is on the verge of being forced out of a very shady side activity. We doubt it ends there.

A significant number of creators, particularly writers, are concerned about the disruptive potential of AI tools such as ChatGPT. Many people believe that artificial intelligence will become an increasingly powerful technology that will assist creators.

Is it a Google Killer?

On the website for OpenAI, it is said that the laboratory is "changing the future of technology." This does not appear to be an example of hyperbole.

OpenAI, which has its headquarters in San Francisco, was established in 2015 by Sam Altman and Elon Musk. Musk withdrew himself in 2018 (though he is still an original funder).

Open AI also counts Microsoft as one of its major donors; in 2019, the software giant contributed one billion dollars to the organization.

The research facility is divided between a non-profit and a commercial division. And the objective that it has set for itself is to create "friendly AI," which is simply artificial intelligence that is beneficial to people in general. Therefore, according to Open AI's official description, their job is not to call the beast.

However, the most pressing issue at hand appears to be determining whether or not Open AI's ChatGPT is, in fact, a viable alternative to Google as many people believe it to be.

It seems that Microsoft is playing a key role in this. It is important to note that the ChatGPT platform is powered by Microsoft's Azure. And for a lot of people, the same can be said about Musk's link to OpenAI.

You may have guessed correctly that the popular opinions on ChatGPT are all over the place. One of these, in particular, piqued our interest.

Those who believe that ChatGPT will be able to displace Google search argue that it will be a lot simpler, more efficient, and more pleasurable way to access all of the information in the world, which is the job that Google currently plays. It would appear that a significant number of people are convinced that Google is up against the most significant challenge to its supremacy in the search industry. If not now, then at some point in the future as bots get more advanced.

And there are other people who are still not sure that ChatGPT will become the dominant language in the world. Or at the very least, not just yet. Some people are simply difficult to impress, and others actively avoid giving the impression that they are impressed by anything. We all know someone like that, whether it's a cousin, a former coworker, or an acquaintance from college.

According to most accounts, the bot has reached a terrifyingly good level now. But it has several problems. It is not very difficult to locate examples online of people citing incorrect or just incorrect search results on ChatGPT. These examples may be found rather easily. Many people object to an AI bot's inability to perform computations, and you can find variations of the claim that an AI bot like ChatGPT is only as effective as the training it receives.

It would appear that there are two different schools of thinking about the danger/opportunity posed by ChatGPT.

A recent post on Yahoo Finance did a good job of presenting these perspectives in a nutshell.

One camp maintains, in essence, that pointing out the problems with ChatGPT is equivalent to judging the application using the incorrect yardstick. Just hold your horses, this debate will continue.

According to Yahoo Finance, this comes from the "just-you-wait" side.

Reza Zadeh, founder and CEO of Matroid, an artificial intelligence computer vision business, as well as an adjunct professor at Stanford University, commented that "part of what's amazing" about ChatGPT is that it generates text that is grammatically acceptable. "This is not something about which they concentrated on ensuring that it was correct. At the moment, it is something that is intended to converse with you while providing responses that are not trivial... When we critique something, it's almost as if we're changing the goalposts.

There is also the "hold your horses" school of thought, which appears to be arguing that it is much too soon to speculate on the eventual destruction of anything due to ChatGPT's influence. Not even Google. Not even close. This point of view, on the other hand, has a tinge of the "at least not yet" feeling to it as well.

This perspective was presented in the Yahoo article by Nima Schei, who is the creator and CEO of Hummimgbirds AI.

"ChatGPT replacing Google Search is like replacing a silo of lemons with a farmer planting lemon trees that potentially becomes a lemon farm – it's possible, but not probable in the short-term," Nima Schei told Yahoo Finance. "It's like replacing a silo of lemons with a farmer planting lemon trees that potentially becomes a lemon farm." "Google

Search has its own benefits, the most notable of which is the quantity of data it possesses as well as the extensive resources it has at its disposal to acquire data. ChatGPT, on the other hand, has a superpower in that it can create human-level bilateral dialogue, which allows it to surpass Google Search's constraints in terms of capturing human intellect.

Have You Considered Competing?

Another thing that's making people anxious about Google's competition with GPT is the fact that Google, which is well-known for its expertise in AI, hasn't created a consumer-facing chatbot that competes with GPT's. And according to what we have read this week, it does not have any immediate intentions to do so, despite the fact that there have been reports of rumblings coming from within Google's own walls.

A recent all-hands meeting at Google was reportedly where employees voiced their concerns about AI to the media outlet CNBC. The piece was published recently. It has been stated that a number of workers have voiced their concern that they are losing ground to other competitors in the field. Executives from Google have reportedly told CNBC that there are currently no plans to release a consumer chatbot similar to OpenAI's ChatGPT in the near future.

Reputational risk was cited as the primary issue voiced by Google executives during an all-hands meeting, according to reports. If they released a bot right now that regularly returned the erroneous answers (like many people claim GPT does), this could cause more problems for Google than it solved. This makes perfect sense in every way. But it is also reminiscent of the old "cannibalization" argument that had Yellow Pages execs twisted in knots while Google took at their firm. This argument stopped Yellow Pages executives from being able to focus on growing their business.

10 Cool Things That You Can Do With ChatGPT

In the last few years, there has been an increasing rise in the number of products that use artificial intelligence. AI writing tools, AI text-to-image generators, and even AI self-portraits have impressed us. Now, ChatGPT, an AI chatbot that is taking the internet by storm, shows us what AI technology can do.

1. Write Jokes (lol)
What would life be without some fun? ChatGPT can be helpful if you want to have a good laugh or make some funny jokes to show off to your friends. Even though AI chatbots aren't usually known for being funny, ChatGPT shows that it could be.

2. Explain the complex
Sometimes, you can't get a clear picture of a subject just by Googling it. Think about wormholes, dark matter, and all those crazy theories you learned about in your Master's program. Or maybe it's a strange sport whose rules you don't understand.

3. Content In Multiple Languages
If you make content and want to reach more people, ChatGPT could help you a lot if you want to make content in more than one language. Yes sure, there's Google Translate, but if you write something in one language and then translate it to another, you might lose a lot of the context and tone of the first language. ChatGPT can make content in several languages right away. Is it Chinese? Yes, I know Spanish. Is it French?

4. Resume Writing Assistant
Writing a personalized resume and cover letter for every job you apply for can be one of the most time-consuming parts of the job application process.

5. Plan for a Job Interview
ChatGPT is one of the best AI tools to help you prepare for a job interview. It has a lot of knowledge in many different areas. You can use it to come up with hypothetical job interview situations, possible questions, smart answers to possible questions, and many other helpful ways to prepare for an interview.

6. How to explain math or even do your math...
ChatGPT is especially good at math problems, whether they are hard algebra problems or simple math problems that are hard to figure out on your own. For the best results, you'll need to explain your problems in a clear and brief way.

7. Advice on Relationships *(replace your therapist)*
ChatGPT, like all AI systems, doesn't really understand how people feel. But it can still help you figure out how to deal with your friends, family, and loved ones. If you ask it the right questions, it can be your personal therapist or relationship expert. (maybe...)

8. You can make music in almost any style.
"Learned creativity" is one of the best things about ChatGPT. ChatGPT is not like some AI solutions that only deal with soulless robot ideas. It also knows how to do creative things, like writing music. You can write almost any song in most of the main types of music. Maybe you can become a recording artist. LMK

9. Writing essays on almost any subject
We strongly recommend that you write your own essays, but ChatGPT can write great essays on a wide range of topics, even the most difficult ones.

10. Chat Partner

ChatGPT is an AI chatbot when all is said and done. Even though it has almost endless uses, ChatGPT is a very helpful friend when you need to talk to someone (or a robot).

DISCLAIMER

Validate Each and Every ChatGPT Result
While ChatGPT is a very accurate AI chatbot, it is nonetheless susceptible to errors. Prior to using ChatGPT, it is vital to verify the accuracy of the information it offers, as its rate of inaccuracy is not alarming.

As a precaution, the information generated by ChatGPT should not be used to make important health or financial decisions without extensive verification. ChatGPT is a game-changing AI product, however it is still mostly under development.

How will you use it?

Let us Help

Check out:
AiBrandAccelerator.com

Chapter #17 Tools & Resources

Tools

Replace over 21 tools with one solution

All-in-One AI-Powered Solution
AiBrandAccelerator.com

ReachOut.AI

Reachout.AI is a personalization platform for automated 1:1 video messaging, preferred by founders and sales teams for breaking through inbox clutter and driving consistent, predictable sales conversations and appointments using the power of A.I. Reachout.ai is an AI-powered video prospecting platform built for busy entrepreneurs and sales teams who love getting high email response rates and starting conversations with prospects—but hate wasting time recording 1:1 videos.

- Stand out in a crowded inbox
- Get the highest CTR you've ever seen!
- Hit industry-shattering reply rates
- Land more meetings with ideal clients
- Automate your video prospecting
- Say goodbye to recording & editing videos

https://reachout.ai/

Synthesia

Create AI-powered videos in minutes. Say goodbye to expensive traditional video creation. AI video creation is a time and cost-efficient alternative to the complex and costly traditional video creation processes.
https://www.synthesia.io/

AI-Powered Paraphraser
https://quillbot.com/

Otter.ai

Automatically capture meeting notes. Find the information you need. Keep everyone informed and aligned.
https://otter.ai/

AI TOOLS

Lex.page
AI text-generation tool.

Copy.ai
AI text-generation tool.

QuillBot
An AI-driven writing tool that paraphrases what you say.

Jasper
AI writing tool

Postwise.ai
AI-driven Twitter writing tool

Craft.do
Document-creation tool with AI features

Canva Docs
Canva launched this tool in the second half of 2022 as a competitor for Google Docs. It includes a few AI tools, including the "Magic" tool that lets you type in a topic and it gives you some text related to that topic. It's good for breaking writer's block.

Google Autodraw
An AI drawing tool that lets you sketch something on the screen and Google's AI will search for rights-free icons that you can download and use. Good for designing logos, too. Just make sure your pop-up blockers are turned off so the icons will appear at the top of the screen.

Google Pinpoint
This tool uses AI to analyze PDFs, strip text from images and transcribe audio.

JournalismAI Starter Pack
A guide designed to help news organizations learn about the opportunities offered by AI to support their journalism.

ChatGPT
Developed by OpenAI in late 2022, the tool interacts in a conversational way. The dialogue format makes it possible for ChatGPT to answer follow-up questions, admit its mistakes, challenge incorrect premises, and reject inappropriate requests.

ChatGPT for Google
Browser extension that allows ChatGPT to work alongside Google.

Awesome ChatGPT Prompts
The ChatGPT model is a large language model trained by OpenAI that is capable of generating human-like text. By providing it with a prompt, it can generate responses that continue the conversation or expand on the given prompt. In this repository, you will find a variety of prompts that can be used with ChatGPT. You can add your own prompts to the list, and to use ChatGPT to generate new prompts as well

LearnGPT
The best ChatGPT examples from around the web.

For current updated list of resources by visit:

AiBrandAccelerator.com/links

Chapter #18
Glossary of Terms

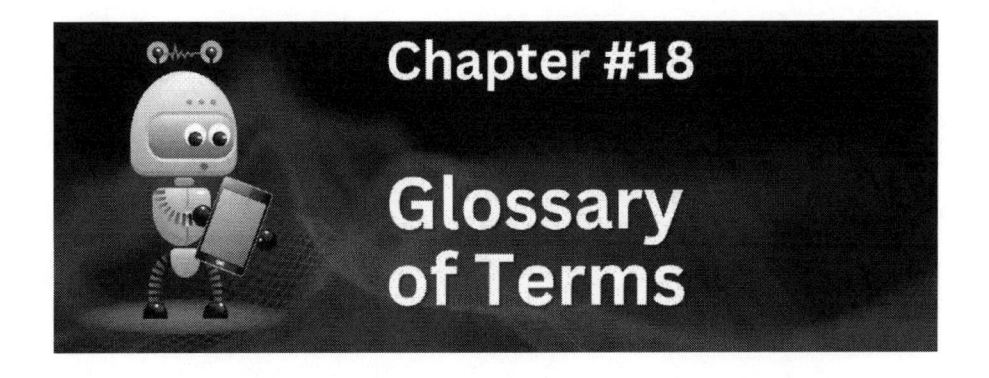

Artificial Intelligence Terms

Artificial intelligence (AI) is a field filled with technical terms. It can be difficult to pin down exactly what a term means, particularly if you don't work directly with data every day.

That's why I created a glossary of 50 AI terms that frequently come up in discussions about AI and machine learning.

Algorithm: A set of rules that a machine can follow to learn how to do a task.

Artificial intelligence: This refers to the general concept of machines acting in a way that simulates or mimics human intelligence. AI can have a variety of features, such as human-like communication or decision making.

Autonomous: A machine is described as autonomous if it can perform its task or tasks without needing human intervention.

Backward chaining: A method where the model starts with the desired output and works in reverse to find data that might support it.

Bias: Assumptions made by a model that simplify the process of learning to do its assigned task. Most supervised machine learning models perform better with low bias, as these assumptions can negatively affect results.

Big data: Datasets that are too large or complex to be used by traditional data processing applications.

Bounding box: Commonly used in image or video tagging, this is an imaginary box drawn on visual information. The contents of the box are labeled to help a model recognize it as a distinct type of object.

Chatbot: A chatbot is program that is designed to communicate with people through text or voice commands in a way that mimics human-to-human conversation.

Cognitive computing: This is effectively another way to say artificial intelligence. It's used by marketing teams at some companies to avoid the science fiction aura that sometimes surrounds AI.

Computational learning theory: A field within artificial intelligence that is primarily concerned with creating and analyzing machine learning algorithms.

Corpus: A large dataset of written or spoken material that can be used to train a machine to perform linguistic tasks.

Data mining: The process of analyzing datasets in order to discover new patterns that might improve the model.

Data science: Drawing from statistics, computer science and information science, this interdisciplinary field aims to use a variety of scientific methods, processes and systems to solve problems involving data.

Dataset: A collection of related data points, usually with a uniform order and tags.

Deep learning: A function of artificial intelligence that imitates the human brain by learning from the way data is structured, rather than from an algorithm that's programmed to do one specific thing.

Entity annotation: The process of labeling unstructured sentences with information so that a machine can read them. This could involve labeling all people, organizations and locations in a document, for example.

Entity extraction: An umbrella term referring to the process of adding structure to data so that a machine can read it. Entity extraction may be done by humans or by a machine learning model.

Forward chaining: A method in which a machine must work from a problem to find a potential solution. By analyzing a range of hypotheses, the AI must determine those that are relevant to the problem.

General AI: AI that could successfully do any intellectual task that can be done by any human being. This is sometimes referred to as *strong AI*, although they aren't entirely equivalent terms.

Hyperparameter: Occasionally used interchangeably with *parameter*, although the terms have some subtle differences. Hyperparameters are values that affect the way your model learns. They are usually set manually outside the model.

Intent: Commonly used in training data for chatbots and other natural language processing tasks, this is a type of label that defines the purpose or goal of what is said. For example, the intent for the phrase "turn the volume down" could be "decrease volume".

Label: A part of training data that identifies the desired output for that particular piece of data.

Linguistic annotation: Tagging a dataset of sentences with the subject of each sentence, ready for some form of analysis or assessment. Common uses for linguistically annotated data include sentiment analysis and natural language processing.

Machine intelligence: An umbrella term for various types of learning algorithms, including machine learning and deep learning.

Machine learning: This subset of AI is particularly focused on developing algorithms that will help machines to learn and change in response to new data, without the help of a human being.

Machine translation: The translation of text by an algorithm, independent of any human involvement.

Model: A broad term referring to the product of AI training, created by running a machine learning algorithm on training data.

Neural network: Also called a *neural net*, a neural network is a computer system designed to function like the human brain. Although researchers are still working on creating a machine model of the human brain, existing neural networks can perform many tasks involving speech, vision and board game strategy.

Natural language generation (NLG): This refers to the process by which a machine turns structured data into text or speech that humans can understand. Essentially, NLG is concerned with what a machine writes or says as the end part of the communication process.

Natural language processing (NLP): The umbrella term for any machine's ability to perform conversational tasks, such as recognizing what is said to it, understanding the intended meaning and responding intelligibly.

Natural language understanding (NLU): As a subset of natural language processing, natural language understanding deals with helping machines to recognize the intended meaning of language — taking into account its subtle nuances and any grammatical errors.

Overfitting: An important AI term, overfitting is a symptom of machine learning training in which an algorithm is only able to work on or identify specific examples present in the training data. A working model should be able to use the general trends behind the data to work on new examples.

Parameter: A variable inside the model that helps it to make predictions. A parameter's value can be estimated using data and they are usually not set by the person running the model.

Pattern recognition: The distinction between pattern recognition and machine learning is often blurry, but this field is basically concerned with finding trends and patterns in data.

Predictive analytics: By combining data mining and machine learning, this type of analytics is built to forecast what will happen within a given timeframe based on historical data and trends.

Python: A popular programming language used for general programming.

Reinforcement learning: A method of teaching AI that sets a goal without specific metrics, encouraging the model to test different scenarios rather than find a single answer. Based on human feedback, the model can then manipulate the next scenario to get better results.

Semantic annotation: Tagging different search queries or products with the goal of improving the relevance of a search engine.

Sentiment analysis: The process of identifying and categorizing opinions in a piece of text, often with the goal of determining the writer's attitude towards something.

Strong AI: This field of research is focused on developing AI that is equal to the human mind when it comes to ability. *General AI* is a similar term often used interchangeably.

Supervised learning: This is a type of machine learning where structured datasets, with inputs and labels, are used to train and develop an algorithm.

Test data: The unlabeled data used to check that a machine learning model is able to perform its assigned task.

Training data: This refers to all of the data used during the process of training a machine learning algorithm, as well as the specific dataset used for training rather than testing.

Transfer learning: This method of learning involves spending time teaching a machine to do a related task, then allowing it to return to its original work with improved accuracy. One potential example of this is taking a model that analyzes sentiment in product reviews and asking it to analyze tweets for a week.

Turing test: Named after Alan Turing, famed mathematician, computer scientist and logician, this tests a machine's ability to pass for a human, particularly in the fields of language and behavior. After being graded by a human, the machine passes if its output is indistinguishable from that of human participant's.

Unsupervised learning: This is a form of training where the algorithm is asked to make inferences from datasets that don't contain labels. These inferences are what help it to learn.

Validation data: Structured like training data with an input and labels, this data is used to test a recently trained model against new data and to analyze performance, with a particular focus on checking for overfitting.

Variance: The amount that the intended function of a machine learning model changes while it's being trained. Despite being flexible, models with high variance are prone to overfitting and low predictive accuracy because they are reliant on their training data.

Variation: Also called *queries* or *utterances*, these work in tandem with intents for natural language processing. The variation is what a person might say to achieve a certain purpose or goal. For example, if the intent is "pay by credit card," the variation might be "I'd like to pay by card, please."

Weak AI: Also called *narrow AI*, this is a model that has a set range of skills and focuses on one particular set of tasks. Most AI currently in use is weak AI, unable to learn or perform tasks outside of its specialist skill set.

Digital Marketing Terms

A/B testing: is when you test two different versions of a marketing campaign to see which delivers better results.

Bottom-of-the-funnel content (BOFU): is content that is created for users that are about to make a purchase. It features sales-driven language and offers things like demos and consultations.

Brand positioning: refers to the way you present yourself to your customers. In turn, it signifies the way that customers connect with your brand based on your values and the way that you stand out from competitors.

Brand awareness: is the level at which users can recall and recognize your brand name. You build brand awareness by being present on social media platforms, sending email newsletters, and appearing in search engines.

Buyer persona: is a fictitious profile that you create to outline your ideal customer. This profile helps you create effective marketing campaigns by imagining how your target persona would like to be marketed to, what profiles they use, and what kind of content they read.

CMS: stands for content management system, and it allows users to create, host, and manage website content. WordPress is an example of a CMS.

Customer acquisition: refers to the process of attracting customers to your business. It includes establishing a relationship with potential customers, showing them that you understand their needs, and providing them with the info they need to convert.

Customer retention: refers to the process of keeping your customers on board with your company by satisfying them with your services.

Churn rate: is also referred to as customer retention and can help you determine how many customers you lose in a specified period.

Customer acquisition cost (CAC): (or patient acquisition cost among medical practices) is how much it costs to turn a lead into a paying customer.

Cost per click (CPC): refers to how much you pay for each one of your clicks on a PPC ad.

Cost per lead (CPL): is how much you spend to acquire a lead.

Cost per thousand (CPM): refers to cost per thousand, which helps you determine how much 1000 views or impressions would cost.

Customer lifetime value (CLV): is how much revenue a specific customer is forecasted to drive for your business.

Click through rate (CTR): is determined by how many times a user clicks on an ad or a link and arrives at the page you're tracking.

Conversion rate: is the percentage of your site's visitors or ad viewers that complete the desired goal, which is typically a conversion or purchase.

Demand generation: is when you create a need for your product using the data you've collected about your target audience and past campaigns.

Direct message: is when a user messages you via a social media platform's private message platform.

Deliverability rate: Also known as acceptance rate, the deliverability rate is the percentage of emails that are accepted by the recipients' email server.

Double opt-in: is when users must complete two actions before subscribing to your email content. For example, a sign-up form and a confirmation link.

Dynamic content: is content that changes within an email based on the subscriber. For example, the content might change based on the age or gender of the subscriber.

Email automation: is when you create personalized emails to send to specific groups of subscribers and automate them to reach recipients at the right time. There is a variety of email automation software on the market. Check out: aibrandaccelerator.com

Email personalization: is when you customize the content of the email based on the subscriber's previous interest, previous actions on your site, age, location, and more.

Email segmentation: is when you segment emails into different buckets based on interests, send times, and more.

Inbound marketing: refers to tactics that target your ideal users instead of marketing to those who might not be interested. Inbound marketing tactics include SEO, social media, content marketing, and more — and refer to tactics that attract your target users rather than you reaching out to them.

Keyword research: is the process of discovering key terms that your target audience uses when searching online. You can use a keyword research tool to help you discover these terms.

Key performance indicator (KPI): help you track your marketing goals' success rate. When you set KPIs for your marketing campaign, you determine what metrics are most important, and track them over time.

Landing page: use forms, images, and organized information to encourage a user to convert. They are where users arrive after clicking an ad.

Marketing automation: allows you to program marketing tasks so that you don't have to do them manually. Marketing automation software makes it easy to nurture leads and boost the efficiency of your marketing campaigns.

Middle-of-the-funnel content (MOFU): is content that you create for users who are about halfway through the buyer journey. This kind of content includes things like case studies or solutions that you provide.

Top-of-the-funnel content (TOFU): caters to users who are just learning about a topic, and not ready to use your services or buy your products. This content is more informational and focused on creating a relationship with potential customers.

Return on ad spend (ROAS): helps you understand how much return you generate in comparison to how much you spend on ads.

Open rate: is the percentage of emails that are opened by recipients.

Transactional email: is an email that is triggered when a customer makes a purchase.

Hard bounce: occurs when an email you send is returned to you based on a wrong email address or an incorrect domain name.

Soft bounce: occurs when a file is too big to send, or the inbox of the person you're sending to is full.

PPC: is a paid strategy that allows you to appear above organic results in search engines. You can target your most qualified audience with keywords in your PPC ads, and you only pay when users click them — not for ranking real estate.

SEO: is the practice of optimizing your website for search engines and users. The end goal of SEO is to help your content rank highly in search engines like Google so that your target audience finds you when they search for a term that you target with your content. SEO helps you rank organically, or without paying for rankings.

Ai BRAND ACCELERATOR

Replace over 21 tools with one solution

All-in-One AI-Powered Solution
AiBrandAccelerator.com

Made in the USA
Columbia, SC
15 May 2023

9a9e9757-e892-4d7e-b497-f3d2ade74511R01